Amazing Facts About Mammals

By

DON BLATTNER

COPYRIGHT © 2006 Mark Twain Media, Inc.

ISBN 1-58037-322-4

Printing No. CD-404052

Mark Twain Media, Inc., Publishers
Distributed by Carson-Dellosa Publishing Company, Inc.

Table of Contents

Introduction iv
Mammals Trivia 1
Mammals Trivia Answers 2
Mammals: North America 4
Mammals: North America Answers 7
Mythbuster: Beavers 9
Mammals: South America 11
Mammals: South America Answers 12
Collective Nouns for Mammals 13
Mammals: Australia 14
Mammals: Australia Answers 16
Australian Coat of Arms Puzzle 17
A Fascinating Fact About a Mammal 18
Mammals: Asia 19
Mammals: Asia Answers 20
Camel Puzzle 21
Mammals: Elephants 22
Mammals: Elephants Answers 24
Amazing Mammals Fact Puzzle 26
Mammals: Hippopotamus and Rhinoceros 28
Mammals: Hippopotamus and Rhinoceros Answers 29
Mammals: Giraffes 30
Mammals: Giraffes Answers 31
Mammals: Old World Monkeys 32
Mammals: Old World Monkeys Answers 34
Odd Mammal Fact From History 36
Mammals: New World Monkeys 38
Mammals: New World Monkeys Answers 39
What's the Difference? 40
Mammals: Chimpanzees 41
Mammals: Chimpanzees Answers 43
Mammals: Gorillas 45
Mammals: Gorillas Answers 46
Animals' Homes 47
Find the Mammals 48
Mammals: Orangutans 49
Mammals: Orangutans Answers 50
Baby Mammals 51
Mammals: Lemurs 52
Mammals: Lemurs Answers 54
Mammals: Lions 55
Mammals: Lions Answers 56

Table of Contents (cont.)

Mammals: Other Big Cats...57
Mammals: Other Big Cats Answers 59
Mythbuster: Rodents 60
Mammals: Bears...63
Mammals: Bears Answers 64
Mammals: Dogs..65
Mammals: Dogs Answers 66
Dog Idioms 67
Mammals: Cats...68
Mammals: Cats Answers 69
Cat Idioms 70
Mammals: Horses...71
Mammals: Horses Answers 73
Horse Idioms 75
Farm Animals 76
Farm Animals Answers 78
Farm Animals Idioms 80
Cow Puzzle...82
Mammals: Bats...83
Mammals: Bats Answers 85
Mythbuster: Bats..87
Mammals: Sea Creatures—Whales 89
Mammals: Sea Creatures—Whales Answers..92
Mammals: Sea Creatures—Sea Otters 95
Mammals: Sea Creatures—Sea Otters Answers 96
Mammals: Sea Creatures—Dolphins 97
Mammals: Sea Creatures—Dolphins Answers..98
Mammals: Other Sea Mammals 99
Mammals: Other Sea Mammals Answers 101
Olympics in the Animal World..103
Olympics in the Animal World Answers 105
Logic Problem: Prairie Mammals...107
Logic Problem: Camel Races 109
Logic Problem: Elephants..110
Logic Problems: Primates..111
Logic Problem: The African Water Hole 112
Logic Problem: Selling Zoo Mammals 112
Logic Problem: Lion Hunt 113
Scientific Mysteries..114
Answers to Activities..115
Amazing Mammals Fact Sheet 123
Bibliography 124

Introduction

Students love to learn about animals. They are especially fond of discovering interesting, bizarre, and often surprising habits of animals. These unusual facts that students enjoy are often considered unimportant and ignored in lesson plans. Here are a few examples.

- Badgers air their bedding in the spring.
- In Ancient Egypt when a pet cat died, the family would shave their eyebrows.
- A polar bear's fur is not white. Its fur is transparent, and its skin is black.
- The Blonde Mangalitza pig is a breed of pig in Hungary that has fleece like a sheep.
- The saliva of vampire bats is being studied as a treatment for stroke.

The second problem in studying mammals is that many of the "facts" we have learned in school or that have been passed down from past generations are either not true or cannot be documented. Some of them may have begun as a story someone told their grandchildren, and the grandchild passed it along, and eventually it was published and became part of folklore. In other cases, stories have been recorded by individuals who either hated or liked certain mammals and purposely lied about them. Here are some examples:

- The hump of a camel is not filled with water. It is filled with fat.
- Bats rarely give humans disease. Like all mammals, they can get rabies, but they do not contract the disease nor spread it any more than other mammals.
- Bats avoid contact with humans. They don't become entangled in a person's hair.
- Gorillas are not ferocious creatures; they are gentle.
- The porcupine does not "shoot" its quills.

This book is designed as a series of quizzes that includes these as well as many other amazing facts about mammals. It doesn't deal with all of the important facts about mammals that students learn in school. Instead, by revealing little-known facts, it gives an unusual and interesting view of many of the creatures that students find fascinating.

The book is especially valuable as a pre-learning activity. Prior to studying a unit, one of the tests from this book should pique a student's interest, arouse his or her curiosity, and give a different perspective to what he or she is about to learn. It will be a springboard for discussion. Just as important as the facts and answers are the explanations after each quiz. The explanations of some of the answers give elaborate details concerning these unusual facts. The answers and explanations are printed just after the questions so they can be duplicated and given to the students for further study.

In addition to the quizzes, there are puzzles and logic problems dealing with mammals. Some are very easy, and others are quite difficult. Also, there is a section called "Scientific Mysteries." These are actual mysteries that the students are invited to solve. They can solve the mystery by themselves, in groups, or the teacher may present the mystery as a twenty-question type of activity. In this case, the teacher would read the mystery to the class, and the students would try to solve it by asking the teacher questions. The teacher can only answer "yes" or "no" to the questions.

Here's one other suggestion. Have your students start their own list of strange and unusual facts about mammals they find in their research. Print the list for your students at the end of the year.

Name: _____ Date: _____

Mammals Trivia

Directions: Indicate if the statements listed below are either "True" or "False" by circling the correct response.

True   False   1. The orca whale is one of the few species of whales that actually comes on shore.

True   False   2. When a horse is born, its legs are almost as long as they will be when it grows up.

True   False   3. About five percent of all mammals can fly.

True   False   4. An elephant keeper sometimes uses a blowtorch in order to clean the animal's hide.

True   False   5. Chimpanzees can swim faster than fish.

True   False   6. In 1916, an elephant was arrested and hanged for murder in Erwin, Tennessee.

True   False   7. Some tribes treat nosebleeds with the smoke from burning giraffe skins.

True   False   8. Giraffe twins have identical patterns of spots.

True   False   9. The giant anteater eats over 10,000,000 ants or termites a year.

True   False   10. Until Europeans arrived, there were no hoofed animals in Australia.

True   False   11. A horse focuses its eye by changing the shape of the lens.

True   False   12. Many years ago in Siam, anyone who displeased the emperor was given a white elephant.

True   False   13. Anteaters are the only mammals to have no teeth.

True   False   14. Sperm whales can stay submerged for up to two days.

True   False   15. A baboon once worked as a signalman for a railway company in South Africa.

True   False   16. Camels are able to close their noses, and alligators are able to close their ears.

True   False   17. Camels have two sets of eyelids.

True   False   18. Meerkats join gangs.

True   False   19. The nine-banded armadillo regularly produces the largest litters of any mammals.

True   False   20. Llamas are used as beasts of burden in the Andes. They carry goods from one place to another. They will refuse to carry anything that weighs more than 50 pounds.

True   False   21. Each day, one species of life becomes extinct.

True   False   22. Red-capped mangabeys, medium-sized, tree-dwelling African monkeys, communicate by using hand signals.

True   False   23. A camel is capable of drinking a bathtub full of water at one time.

True   False   24. An elephant will sometimes use a large stick held in its trunk in order to remove an infected tooth.

True   False   25. The Hanuman langur is an Asian monkey. One of its favorite foods contains strychnine, a poison that will kill a human.

1

Mammals Trivia Answers

1. True. Orcas intentionally beach themselves in Argentina and the Crozet Islands in order to capture a baby sea lion. They go onto the beach by using their front flippers, grab the sea lion, and then roll back into the ocean. The orca does not eat the sea lion immediately, but will toss it into the air several times as a lesson for young orcas.
2. True.
3. False. The nearly 1,000 species of bats comprise almost 25 percent of all known mammals by species.
4. True.
5. False. Chimpanzees hate water. They will go miles out of their way to go around a small river, rather than wade across it. When it rains, a chimp becomes depressed and bows his head until the rain stops.
6. True. The elephant's name was Big Mary, and she worked with a circus that was performing in Tennessee. One day her trainer poked her with a stick, and Big Mary stomped on him. The circus decided that people would not come to the circus as long as Big Mary was around, so they decide to execute her. The problem was, "How do you kill an elephant?" Guns used by hunters were not powerful enough to do the job. Someone suggested hanging the elephant with a crane owned by the railroad yard located in nearby Erwin. Thousands of people showed up for the hanging. They locked a chain around Big Mary's neck and then raised the crane. The chain broke and Big Mary fell and was knocked unconscious. They quickly put the chain around her neck again, and this time they were successful.
7. True.
8. False. No two giraffes have the same pattern of spots. No two zebras have the same pattern of stripes.
9. True.
10. True. Cattle, horses, goats, deer, and other hoofed animals were all imported.
11. False. Unlike humans who change the shape of their lens, a horse focuses its eye by changing the angle of its head.
12. True. Thailand was once called Siam. Many years ago in Siam, white elephants, which are rare, were considered sacred. If one was found, it was given to the emperor. In fact, the emperor was known as the "Lord of the White Elephant." It is recorded that if the emperor became angry with one of his nobles, he would send that noble a white elephant. Since the elephant was sacred, the noble could not destroy it. He couldn't give it away, since it was a gift from the emperor. So, he had to take care of it. The cost of maintaining an elephant is extremely high. Eventually, the noble used up all his money and resources in taking care of the elephant and became poor. Over the years, the phrase "white elephant" has come to mean items that are expensive but useless.
13. True.
14. False. Sperm whales breathe air and can only stay submerged for up to two hours. They can dive over a mile below the surface of the water.
15. True. James Wilde was a guard working on a South African railway when he slipped, fell under a train, and lost both legs. As a result of this accident, Wilde could no longer work as a guard for the railway and became unemployed. He made himself pegged-legs and also a wagon-like contraption that enabled him to get around. So, the railway company hired him to be a signalman. One day he went to the marketplace and met a man who had a baboon.

Mammals Trivia Answers (cont.)

James was able to buy the baboon and taught him to push him in his wagon to and from work.

The baboon had only been with James at the railway a few days when it began imitating James' jobs. James was impressed with its intelligence, so he trained the baboon to listen to the length and number of blasts from the train's whistles that told the signalman how to change the signals. He also taught him other parts of his job. Eventually, the baboon was able to do everything James was able to do. He did everything quickly and accurately.

That should be the end of the story, but it isn't. One day someone saw the baboon changing the signals, thought it was a dangerous thing, and reported it. The baboon was fired. James and the other workers at the railway begged the authorities to give the baboon a test to prove he was reliable. They agreed and made up a very difficult test with signals that were changed quickly and often. The baboon responded to every signal correctly. The authorities gave him his job back.

The baboon was named Jack the Signalman. He was given an employment number and a monthly ration from the government. He was paid 20 cents a day and a half a bottle of beer on Saturdays. He worked for nine years before he died. Over that time, he never made a mistake.

16. True.
17. False. Camels have three sets of eyelids.
18. True. Actually, the group name for meerkats is "gang." Sometimes, for their protection, a gang of meerkats will work together. They will stand up on their hind legs and then advance forward together. Their appearance together is so frightening that even large predators retreat.
19. False. That honor goes to the tailless tenrec, also known as the Madagascar hedgehog. It produces the largest litters of any mammals—as many as 32 babies at once. The nine-banded armadillo always gives birth to quadruplets of the same sex.
20. True.
21. False. It is estimated that each day, anywhere from 35–150 species of life become extinct.
22. False. They use facial expressions. Mangabeys have white eyelids that can easily be seen in the dim light of the forest. The white facial highlights allow these monkeys to "talk" to each other over a long distance.
23. True.
24. True. The molars of an elephant are huge. Its tusks, which are actually teeth, can be over ten feet long. When an elephant has an infected tooth, he is in great pain and will do about anything to get rid of the pain. He might use a stick to remove the tooth, or he might wedge the tusk in the crotch of a tree and pull.
25. True. The Hanuman langur is able to eat tough food that other creatures can't digest. They sometimes eat seeds with high levels of strychnine and other poisons.

Name: _____ Date: _____

Mammals: North America

North America includes Canada, Greenland, the United States, Mexico, Central America, and the islands of the Caribbean Sea. It is the third-largest continent when measured by area. North America has the most varied kind of climate and terrain of any continent. It has warm Caribbean beaches in the south and ice-covered plains in the north. Its landscape has mountains, flat grasslands, deserts, and rain forests. North America has the largest island in the world, as well as the largest freshwater lake. This variety of climates and terrain is the home for some amazing animals.

Directions: Circle the letter of the correct answer(s).

1. The nine-banded armadillo always gives birth to:
   A. Only one newborn at a time.
   B. Identical twins.
   C. Identical triplets.
   D. Identical quadruplets.

2. Armadillos are able to:
   A. Walk on water.
   B. Walk underwater.
   C. Fly from tree to tree.
   D. Go without water for three weeks.

3. The common nine-banded armadillo is used in research to find a cure for:
   A. Psoriasis.   B. Leprosy.
   C. Cancer.   D. Baldness.

4. In the spring, badgers:
   A. Mate.   B. Air their bedding.
   C. Hibernate.   D. Migrate to the north.

5. Beavers build their lodges in a lake. In order to protect themselves from predators, they protect the entrance by:
   A. Building it underwater.   B. Rolling a stone in front of it.
   C. Building it near a snake hole. D. Closing it with mud.

6. What is the largest deer in the world?
   A. Reindeer   B. The Alaskan bull moose
   C. Thompson Gazelle   D. Le John Deer

7. In order to protect itself from predators, the hedgehog:
   A. Runs away.   B. Puts poison on its quills.
   C. Fights.   D. Hides in a tree.

4

Name: _____ Date: _____

Mammals: North America (cont.)

8. When a North American opossum is approached by a predator, it:
   A. Pretends to be dead.
   B. Passes out from terror.
   C. Falls asleep.
   D. Begins to meditate.

9. Mice like to:
   A. Dance.
   B. Sing.
   C. Hum.
   D. Draw.

10. When Canadian porcupines greet each other, they:
    A. Hug.
    B. Kiss each other on the lips.
    C. Give each other a "high five."
    D. Wink.

11. If you inject a rabbit with the blood of a sleeping rabbit, it will:
    A. Go to sleep.
    B. Die.
    C. Become immune to certain diseases.
    D. Become a super rabbit.

12. The act of giving birth to a litter of rabbits is called:
    A. Breaking.
    B. Birthing.
    C. Bundling.
    D. Kindling.

13. You can have a general idea where a jackrabbit lives by measuring its:
    A. Teeth.
    B. Fur.
    C. Ears.
    D. Feet.

14. The mole rat lives like a(n):
    A. Mouse.
    B. Guinea pig.
    C. Bee.
    D. Opossum.

15. If there is no water to drink, the North American kangaroo rat:
    A. Will die.
    B. Can live without water.
    C. Will hibernate.
    D. Can survive only six weeks.

16. A dormouse is a sleeper, or hibernator. The dormouse that begins its winter sleep before the others:
    A. May be eaten by the others.
    B. Will lose all of its food.
    C. Will wake up last.
    D. Will wake up first.

17. The yellow-footed marsupial mouse escapes the notice of flying predators by:
    A. Pretending to be dead.
    B. Disguising itself as a leaf.
    C. Walking upside down.
    D. Attaching itself to a bear.

Name: _____ Date: _____

Mammals: North America (cont.)

18. It is possible for a pair of mice to be responsible for this number of offspring in less than a year.
    A. 150
    B. 1,500
    C. 15,000
    D. 150,000

19. For which of the following does a squirrel *not* use its tail?
    A. Sunshade
    B. Third arm
    C. Blanket
    D. Umbrella

20. In the winter, the short-tailed weasel is called a(n):
    A. Mink.
    B. Snow weasel.
    C. Blizzard Bailey.
    D. Ermine.

21. Prairie dogs are a type of large, burrowing squirrel that is native to the western United States. They identify one another by:
    A. Kissing.
    B. Smell.
    C. Touch.
    D. The way they eat.

22. Which of the following rooms is *not* found in a mole's house?
    A. Honeymoon room
    B. Bathroom
    C. Kitchen
    D. Storeroom

23. The scientific name for a wolverine means:
    A. Glutton.
    B. Female wolf.
    C. Smelly weasel.
    D. Brown bear.

24. What fell on Bergen, Norway, in 1578?
    A. Green toads
    B. Lightning balls
    C. Fish
    D. Yellow mice

25. The rodent known as the woodchuck is also called the:
    A. Woodie.
    B. Chuckie.
    C. Little Beaver.
    D. Whistle-pig.

Mammals: North America Answers

1. **D. Identical quadruplets.** Armadillos are burrowing animals whose bodies are enclosed in bony plates. There are several types of armadillos that live from the southern part of the United States to Argentina. While some mammals have lots of babies at once, the nine-banded armadillo always gives birth to quadruplets of the same sex. The babies are identical because they are all formed from a single egg.

2. **B. Walk underwater.** When an armadillo comes to water, it cannot swim because its armored plates are too heavy. So, it usually holds its breath and continues to walk. It will cross the stream or pond while walking on the bottom underwater. It is also possible for some armadillos to gulp down enough air into their digestive systems so they will float.

3. **B. Leprosy.** The common nine-banded armadillo is as susceptible to leprosy as humans are, so it is used to research the disease.

4. **B. Air their bedding.**

5. **A. Building it underwater.** Beavers might be considered architectural geniuses. They prefer to build their homes in lakes, but if there is no lake available, they will build a lake. They find a stream and then, using their very sharp teeth, they gnaw through small trees, which they use to build a dam. They use rocks to secure the trees and other vegetation, and then they seal the dam using mud. The dam can be as high as 10 feet and as long as 100 feet. The beaver then builds its home, called a lodge, in the water. The lodge is built in the shape of a dome using twigs, reeds, stone, and mud. Part of the lodge is underwater, and part is above water. Inside, the beaver builds a platform for sleeping that is above the water's level. The entrance to the lodge is built underwater so that in order to enter, they have to swim in. This design protects the beaver from predators. Beavers adjust the level of the lake by widening the spillways when the lake gets too high and narrowing the spillways when the lake gets too low.

6. **B. The Alaskan bull moose.** They have been known to weigh 1,800 pounds and grow to 7 feet at the shoulders.

7. **B. Puts poison on its quills.** Hedgehogs are covered with spines except for on their faces, legs, and bellies. A hedgehog may have 8,000 spines. In order to protect itself, a hedgehog will either eat or lick a poisonous toad or plant, foam at the mouth, and then lick the poison onto its quills. When attacked, the hedgehog will curl up into a ball with its poisonous spines facing outward. While there are similarities between porcupines and hedgehogs, the two are not related. Hedgehogs are sometimes kept as pets. They eat insects, mice, snails, lizards, frogs, and even snakes.

8. **B. Passes out from terror.** The American opossum is a marsupial. Most pouched animals are found in Australia. The American opossum is the only one found in North America. They are quite small when they are born. About 24 newborns would fit into a teaspoon. As a defense mechanism, when the North American opossum is approached by a predator, it closes its eyes and becomes totally limp. It looks as if it is dead. In fact, when someone is pretending to be asleep, people say he is "playing possum." Many believe an opossum uses this as a trick to make its predator believe that it is dead. In fact, it's not pretending at all. It really does pass out from sheer terror.

9. **B. Sing.** Scientists have actually made recordings of mice singing, whistling, twittering, and chirping like birds. In the 1940s, Americans listened to a radio concert of a mouse singing.

Mammals: North America Answers (cont.)

10. **B. Kiss each other on the lips.** A porcupine has more than 30,000 quills. These quills are hollow and enable a porcupine to float and swim. When threatened, the porcupine will puff up its quills, which makes it look unappetizing. If this does not prevent a predator from attacking, a porcupine will use its tail to push the quills into its enemy. Porcupine quills are not only painful, they are hard to remove because they have little hooks on them that point backward and tear the skin when a person tries to pull them out. When a porcupine is born, however, its quills are soft and mostly white. Within a few hours, they harden.

11. **A. Go to sleep.**

12. **D. Kindling.**

13. **C. Ears.** The longer the jackrabbit's ears, the warmer the place where it lives.

14. **C. Bee.** The naked mole rat is a mammal that burrows. Its colony behaves very much like that of a bee. The mole is ruled by a queen and lives in colonies underground. The queen is the only one of the colony that gives birth to the young. All of the other mole rats perform all of the jobs that are required by the queen. They dig tunnels, find food, look after the young, and generally behave in a manner similar to bees.

15. **B. Can live without water.** North American kangaroo rats can do things of which few other animals are capable. Not only can they survive in temperatures of over 120° Fahrenheit, they can live without ever drinking water. It is not that they don't need water, but their bodies are able to control their water balance. First, they reserve their water loss by staying underground when it is very hot. Second, most of the moisture that the kangaroo rat needs comes from inside its own body. This is called *metabolic water* and is released when the food the rat eats is digested.

16. **A. May be eaten by the others.** When a dormouse hibernates, he really hibernates. A hibernating dormouse can be rolled across a table or tossed in the air, and it won't wake up. When the hibernation period begins, a dormouse must be wary not to be the first one to go to sleep. Other dormice may eat the first one that begins its hibernation before the rest. A dormouse may even devour its own mother if she falls asleep first.

17. **C. By walking upside down.** It walks upside down on a twig.

18. **C. 15,000.**

19. **B. Third arm.**

20. **D. Ermine.**

21. **A. Kissing**

22. **C. Kitchen.**

23. **A. Glutton.** The wolverine is an unusual animal that lives in the Arctic and sub-Arctic regions. It will eat small mammals, or it will scavenge dead animals that others have killed. The name would lead one to believe that the animal was a species of wolf. But it isn't. It looks kind of like a bear, but actually is a member of the weasel family. It was given its scientific name of "glutton" because it attacks and eats any prey with which it comes into contact.

24. **D. Yellow mice.**

25. **D. Whistle-pig.**

Name: _____ Date: _____

Mythbuster: Beavers

Directions: Shown on the following page are a number of questions and statements concerning beavers. Fill in the spaces with the correct word that goes with the statement. Then take the letters in the circles and put them in the spaces below the puzzle. The words that are spelled from these letters explain a myth about beavers.

1.
2.
3.
4.
5.
6.
7.
8.
9.
10.
11.
12.
13.
14.
15. 
16.
17.

ANSWER: ___ __ ___ _____ ___ ___ ___ ____ ____ ___ _____.

Name: _____ Date: _____

Mythbuster: Beavers (cont.)

1. The color of a beaver's fur is reddish- _____.

2. The skin of a beaver with the fur or hair still on it is called a(n) _____

3. Beavers belong to this group of animals that are covered with hair or fur and feed their
    young milk. Most animals in this group give birth to live babies.

4. A person who is overly enthusiastic is called a(n) _____. (Two words)

5. A beaver's home is called a(n) _____.

6. This is one of two states that has the beaver as the state animal. (one word)

7. Beaver dams slow the swift flow of rivers or streams and eliminate the wearing away of the
    soil, which is called _____.

8. This part of the beaver is used for steering, balance, warning signals, and fat storage.

9. Beavers always live near this.

10. These are capable of growing four feet a year and enable the beaver to cut down thick
    trees.

11. This is the second of two states that has the beaver as the state animal (two words)

12. An order of animals that includes beavers, rats, and mice

13. A baby beaver is called a(n) _____.

14. Beavers are strong swimmers because their feet are _____.

15. The beaver was almost hunted to extinction because people wanted its _____.

16. Beavers can get around in the water because they are excellent _____.

17. This is what a group of beavers is called.

Name: _____ Date: _____

Mammals: South America

South America is the fourth-largest continent in area. Like North America, it has nearly every type of landscape and climate. The world's largest tropical rain forest grows in the Amazon River Basin, which makes up about 40 percent of the continent. The Atacama Desert in northern Chile is one of the driest places in the world. Snowy mountain peaks and active volcanoes are part of the Andes Mountains in western South America. South America is a unique continent with unique animals.

Directions: Circle the letter of the correct answer(s).

1. The sloth is an animal that spends most of its life:
   A. In the water.   B. Hunting for food.
   C. Upside down.   D. Building nests.

2. A sloth comes down out of a tree once a week to:
   A. Eat.   B. Drink.   C. Build a nest.   D. Go to the bathroom.

3. If there are too many cool and cloudy days in a row, a sloth may:
   A. Starve to death.   B. Hibernate.
   C. Mate.   D. Move.

4. When it rains, the sloth:
   A. Hides under leaves.   B. Turns green.
   C. Sleeps with its mouth open.   D. Mates.

5. How long is the tongue of the giant anteater of South America?
   A. 10 inches   B. 14 inches   C. 24 inches   D. 34 inches

6. Which of the following does a collared peccary not eat?
   A. Dirt   B. Young peccaries
   C. Cactus   D. Mice

7. What sound does a collared peccary make?
   A. Laugh   B. Rattling   C. Cough   D. Bark

8. The sloth is about the size of a dog. In prehistoric times, there was a giant sloth that was about the size of a(n):
   A. Pony.   B. Horse.   C. Rhinoceros.   D. Elephant

9. When a llama is angry, it will:
   A. Lie down.   B. Spit.   C. Spit stones.   D. Bite.

10. Which of the following are llamas trained to do?
    A. Guard sheep   B. Provide rides at beaches
    C. Participate in basketball games D. Plant corn

11

Mammals: South America Answers

1. **C. Upside down.** There are five different species of sloths that live in South and Central America. Two of the better-known species are the two-toed sloth and the three-toed sloth. A sloth will spend most of its days in trees, eating leaves, sunning itself, and resting upside down. It is able to do this because of its big, hooklike toes. A sloth usually hangs from a branch, with all four feet together and with its head tucked in so it looks like a clump of dead leaves. A sloth's fur even grows down, instead of up. Its hair is parted on its stomach. The sloth spends about 21 hours a day sleeping. It is so slow-moving that it moves at about 1/2 mph and less than 45 yards each day.

2. **D. Go to the bathroom.** The sloth feeds on leaves and fruits. Its teeth are always growing but are worn down by eating. Sloths don't drink but get their water from eating leaves and drinking the dew on the leaves. Once a week, the sloth slowly crawls down to the bottom of the tree in which he is living in order to go to the bathroom. This will fertilize the tree in which it lives.

3. **A. Starve to death.** Even though there may be plenty of food available, a sloth may die if it is cool and cloudy for many days. The sloth must sun itself every day in order to raise its body temperature so that the bacteria in its stomach are warm enough to break down the leaves it eats. It can take 100 hours to digest a stomach full of food.

4. **B. Turns green.** The sloth moves so slowly that green algae actually grows on its coat. The algae turns green when it rains. This allows the sloth to blend in with its leafy surroundings and protects it from predators. When the weather is dry, the algae turns brown so the sloth blends in with the tree trunk.

5. **C. 24 inches.** As its name implies, the giant anteater mainly eats ants, but it also eats termites. Anteaters inhabit the areas from northern Paraguay and Argentina to southern Mexico. It is a toothless creature that has a long tail, curved claws, and a long muzzle that has a small opening. The giant anteater uses its sharp claws to tear open insect nests. It uses its long, sticky tongue to catch about 35,000 ants a day.

6. **B. Young peccaries.** A collared peccary looks like a pig. It has four hoofed toes on its front feet, and three on its hind feet. It has a short snout like a pig. The collared peccary is an *omnivore* because it eats both plants and animals. A peccary mainly eats plants such as seeds, fruit, roots, cacti, and tubers. Sometimes it will eat insects and rodents. Occasionally, the peccary eats dirt for minerals.

7. **A, B, C, D.** Peccaries are pig-like mammals found in the southern parts of the United States to South America. They look like wild pigs. They laugh during squabbles, make rattling sounds with their feet when they are disturbed, cough in order to bring the group together, and emit a barking sound to sound an alarm.

8. **D. Elephant.**

9. **A, B, C, D.** Llamas will lie down and refuse to carry anything that weighs more than 50 pounds. They may also spit, spit stones, or bite when angry.

10. **A. Guard sheep.** Llamas were once native to North America, but eventually migrated to South America. For several decades, farmers in North America have been raising llamas along with their other livestock. Some farmers have pastured llamas with sheep and have been surprised to learn that fewer sheep were being lost to coyotes. Today, many farmers in North America use them as guard animals.

Name: _____ Date: _____

Collective Nouns for Mammals

Some nouns refer to a single animal. Examples would include *cow*, *dog*, or *bird*. There are other nouns that refer to a group of animals. These are called *collective nouns*. Examples would include a *herd*, *pack*, or *flock*. Many of these collective nouns are obvious and well known. Others are very unusual. Some groups of animals are referred to with several different collective nouns. A group of fish, for example, might be called a *school*, *catch*, *run*, *shoal*, *haul*, or *drought*.

Directions: Listed below are a number of animals. At the bottom of the page are collective nouns for these animals. Write the collective noun in the blank opposite the animal to which it refers.

1. Apes _____
2. Baboons _____
3. Bears _____
4. Buffalo _____
5. Camels _____
6. Cats _____
7. Cheetahs _____
8. Chicks _____
9. Colts _____
10. Dolphins _____
11. Elk _____
12. Ferrets _____
13. Foxes _____
14. Giraffes _____
15. Greyhounds _____
16. Goats _____
17. Gorillas _____
18. Hamsters _____

19. Hippopotami _____
20. Hogs _____
21. Jackrabbits _____
22. Kangaroos _____
23. Leopards _____
24. Lions _____
25. Monkeys _____
26. Ponies _____
27. Porpoises _____
28. Puppies _____
29. Rats _____
30. Rhinoceroses _____
31. Seals _____
32. Squirrels _____
33. Swine _____
34. Tigers _____
35. Wolves _____
36. Zebra _____

Use these words: Ambush, Band, Bloat, Brood, Business, Clutter, Coalition, Colony, Crash, Drey, Drift, Flange, Flock, Gang, Harem, Herd, Horde, Husk, Leap, Leash, Litter, Mob, Pack, Pod, Pride, Rag, School, Shrewdness, Skulk, Sleuth, Sounder, String, Tower, Tribe, Troop, Zeal

13

Name: _____ Date: _____

Mammals: Australia

Many of the animals that live in Australia are unique. They are completely different from the animals that live on any other continent. Why are they so different? The answer lies in the fact that Australia is isolated from the rest of the world by a great ocean. Scientists tell us that in prehistoric times there was just one continent in the world. It was called Pangaea. The plants and animals on Pangaea intermingled and evolved together. At some point, however, this large continent broke in two, and one of these parts broke apart even further, and they all drifted apart. Since Australia has been separated from the rest of the world for so long, the plants and animals living there no longer had contact with those from other parts of the world, so they evolved separately. As a consequence, they are completely different from those found on other continents. It is estimated that in Australia approximately 95% of the mammals, 70% of the birds, 88% of the reptiles, and 94% of the frogs are unique and are not found anywhere else.

Directions: Circle the letter of the correct answer(s).

1. The only mammal that has poison glands is the:
   A. Maned wolf.
   C. Killer mole.
   B. Aardvark.
   D. Duck-billed platypus.

2. The duck-billed platypus uses its snout to:
   A. Root for mushrooms.
   C. Pry open clams.
   B. Detect electricity.
   D. Snorkel.

3. The platypus's tail stores up to fifty percent of the animal's:
   A. Blood.
   C. Fat.
   B. Organs.
   D. Sweat glands.

4. When kangaroos are born, they are:
   A. One inch long.
   C. Five pounds.
   B. Twelve inches long.
   D. 25 pounds.

5. A kangaroo can only jump if:
   A. It is above 70°F.
   C. Its tail is touching the ground.
   B. It is over five feet tall.
   D. It is a male.

6. Unlike other four-legged mammals, kangaroos cannot:
   A. Nurse their young.
   C. Be trained to do tricks.
   B. Give birth to a live baby.
   D. Walk backwards.

14

Name: _____ Date: _____

Mammals: Australia (cont.)

7. Until Europeans came to Australia, the country had no:
   A. Snakes.
   B. Bats.
   C. Hoofed animals.
   D. Boomerangs.

8. A person can tell one species of large kangaroo from another by its:
   A. Color.
   B. Feet.
   C. Nose.
   D. Eyebrows.

9. An adult female kangaroo is called a:
   A. Maizie.
   B. Jenny.
   C. Flyer.
   D. Sheila.

10. An adult male kangaroo is called a:
    A. Joseph.
    B. Hopper.
    C. Riley.
    D. Boomer.

11. A young kangaroo is called a:
    A. Bobby.
    B. Joey.
    C. Billy.
    D. Nonny.

12. The koala bear eats only:
    A. Eucalyptus leaves.
    B. Kangaroo eggs.
    C. Koka koala.
    D. Honey.

13. A female koala is pregnant for:
    A. 3–5 days.
    B. 35 days.
    C. 3.5 months.
    D. 3.5 years.

14. The word *koala* may come from an aboriginal word meaning:
    A. Little bear.
    B. No drink.
    C. Forest boy.
    D. Tree bear.

15. Koalas and most other marsupials live in Australia and neighboring islands. The only marsupial native to the United States is the:
    A. Raccoon.
    B. Virginia opossum.
    C. Kangaroo rat.
    D. Brown bear.

16. Koalas smell like:
    A. Cough drops.
    B. Ovaltine.
    C. Mint.
    D. Sulphur.

17. Australia has the largest population of wild _____ in the world.
    A. Alligators.
    B. Sloths.
    C. Camels.
    D. Llamas.

Mammals: Australia Answers

1. **D. Duck-billed platypus.** The duck-billed platypus has spurs on its hind feet, which are used to deliver poison when it kicks an enemy. While the poison is not strong enough to kill a human, it can make a person sick and can kill a small animal.

2. **B. Detect electricity.** The platypus hunts by using its sensitive bill, which has thousands of small openings like pores that have cells that detect small electrical impulses made by the moving muscles of its prey. Electrical impulses are what enable muscles to contract.

3. **C. Fat.** This fat reserve provides the platypus with an energy reserve when food becomes scarce.

4. **A. One inch long.** Kangaroos have short pregnancies, and as a consequence, the newborns are very small—about the size of a peanut. After it is born, the tiny baby crawls up to the mother's belly and into her pouch. Once in the pouch, it attaches itself to the mother's nipple and remains for a long time. From time to time, the mother will clean the inside of the pouch with her lips and will sometimes hold the pouch open with her front paws.

5. **C. Its tail is touching the ground.** The kangaroo's hind legs are shaped like a "Z". Its tail acts almost like another leg balancing it as it hops. When a kangaroo is resting, its weight is balanced by the tripod formed by the hind legs and the tail. A kangaroo jumps forward. It does not jump upward. A large kangaroo can leap as far as 25 feet. A kangaroo's forelegs are short and not used for jumping. Large kangaroos use their forelegs for fighting or playing, while smaller species use them to pick up food to eat.

6. **D. Walk backwards.**

7. **C. Hoofed animals.**

8. **C. Nose.** A red kangaroo's nose is small and has a boomerang-shaped black bare patch. The grey kangaroo's nose is covered with hair. A wallaroo's nose has a large black bare patch around it.

9. **C. Flyer.**

10. **D. Boomer.**

11. **B. Joey.** Most of the joey's growth and development takes place in its mother's pouch.

12. **A. Eucalyptus leaves.**

13. **B. 35 days.**

14. **B. No drink.** Though koalas look like teddy bears and are sometimes even referred to as "koala bears," they are not bears. Koalas do drink when necessary, but they get most of the liquid they need from leaves.

15. **B. Virginia opossum.** The only marsupial native to the United States is the Virginia opossum, which is sometimes called *possum*.

16. **A. Cough drops.** Eucalyptus is a chief ingredient in many cough drops. It is also the entire diet of koalas.

17. **C. Camels.** The only dromedary camels that now exist in the wild are domesticated camels that escaped or that have been freed. These are known as **feral** animals. The camels were originally introduced to Australia in the middle of the nineteenth century as pack animals. Camels performed well in the Australian desert. They were able to carry heavy loads over large, arid distances with little food or water. When railroads, automobiles, and trucks came into popular use, the camels were released to make it on their own. It is estimated that today there may be as many as 700,000 feral camels in Australia.

Name: _____ Date: _____

Frame letters (top, left-to-right): E Y N T A I W L S I D

Frame letters (right side, top-to-bottom): D B R A A P W A K C C E

Frame letters (bottom, left-to-right): K H I A N S G T B H A

Frame letters (left side, top-to-bottom): E O I F T W H A E L R K

Australian Coat of Arms Puzzle

The Australian Coat of Arms was granted in 1912 by King George V. The coat of arms includes a shield that has six sections, with each section containing a symbol for each state. The shield is supported by two Australian animals. The emu is on the right, and the kangaroo is on the left. The question is, "Why were these two animals chosen to appear on the coat of arms?" Certainly they are animals that are native and unique to Australia, but so are many others. It is a commonly held belief that these two animals were chosen because of a specific characteristic. What is it? The answer is hidden in the frame around the picture of the coat of arms shown above. To discover the answer, you must go around the frame twice, reading every other letter. Where do you start, and which way do you read around the frame? That's what you have to figure out.

Answer: _____

Name: _____ Date: _____

A Fascinating Fact About a Mammal

Directions: Do you want to learn a fascinating fact about a mammal? It is hidden in the group of words at the bottom of the page. You'll find it by eliminating all of the words that are not a part of the fact. The following list will direct you to cross out the words that are not a part of the fact. Once all of the extra words are eliminated, unscramble the sentence in order to discover the amazing fact.

Cross out the following from the words at the bottom of the page:

1. Biggest animal in the world
2. Tallest animal in the world
3. Found on sheep
4. What a baby cat is called
5. Ivory is taken from these three animals.
6. The animal people say is sly
7. Three islands
8. Where many penguins live
9. Often confused with a turtle
10. A member of the dog family
11. A member of the cat family from South America
12. The body of this animal is enclosed in bony plates.
13. Three primates
14. Two beasts of burden
15. What a group of cattle is called
16. A flying mammal
17. Six farm animals
18. Favorite food of a polar bear
19. What pandas eat
20. The only North American marsupial
21. Where a baby kangaroo lives
22. Three rivers

A ages Amazon Antarctica armadillo at bamboo bat blue whale boar camel can Cayman chicken chimpanzee Cook cow coyote different different duck elephant female Fiji fleece fox giraffe goose gorilla herd is jaguar kangaroo kinds kitten milk Mississippi monkey Nile nursing of of opossum ox pig pouch produce same seal she sheep the time tortoise two walrus when youngsters

Unscramble the remaining words to form a sentence and discover the amazing fact.

_____

_____

_____

Name: _____ Date: _____

Mammals: Asia

Asia is the largest of the earth's seven continents. It lies almost entirely in the Northern Hemisphere. With outlying islands, it covers about 30% of the world's total land area. It has very exotic animals. You will notice that several well-known Asian animals, such as pandas, elephants, orangutans, and others are not included in the questions below. Questions about these animals are included in other sections of this workbook.

**Binturong
(Asian bearcat)**

Directions: Circle the letter of the correct answer(s).

1. The hump of a camel contains:
   A. Water.   B. Cartilage.   C. Fat.   D. Milk.

2. A camel's backbone is:
   A. Curved.   B. Straight.   C. Made of gristle.   D. A sac filled with water.

3. Which of the following can go the longest without water?
   A. Camel   B. Llama   C. Rat   D. Whale

4. Which of the following is *not* a use for camel's hair?
   A. Artists' brushes   B. Coats   C. Wigs   D. Tents

5. Camels originated in:
   A. North America.   B. Asia.   C. Africa.   D. Australia.

6. The tail of a fat-tail sheep is so big that:
   A. It is carried around on a cart.   B. It develops calluses from being dragged.
   C. Its young is carried on it.   D. It does not fit in the sheep's stall.

7. The fur of the binturong, also known as the Asian bearcat, smells like:
   A. A dead skunk.   B. Popcorn   C. Tobacco smoke   D. Bananas

8. From what animal do we get the luxuriously soft wool known as cashmere?
   A. Goat   B. Sheep   C. Bat   D. Camel

9. What is a zebu?
   A. Part zebra, part horse   B. Part zebra, part walrus
   C. A relative of the cow   D. A word game

10. The binturong uses its tail as a(n):
    A. Umbrella   B. Weapon   C. Blanket   D. Brake

11. The civet, a catlike animal found in Africa and Asia, drives off its enemies with a foul-smelling spray. This spray is used in the manufacturing of:
    A. A spray to stop criminals.   B. Cheese.
    C. Perfume.   D. Furniture polish.

Mammals: Asia Answers

1. **C. Fat.** Many people believe that a camel stores water in its hump. It doesn't. The camel's hump(s) actually stores flesh and fat, which the camel uses as nutrition when food is scarce. When a camel uses its fat in its hump for nutrition, the mound shrinks and becomes flabby. If a camel uses too much of the fat in its hump, the hump will not only shrink, it will flop and hang down the camel's side. After resting and eating, the hump will return to its normal up-right condition.

2. **B. Straight.**

3. **C. Rat.**

4. **C. Wigs.** When camels molt in the spring, they will shed about five pounds of hair. A new coat will be grown by autumn. Camel hair is used in many products such as high-quality coats, clothing, tents, rugs, and artists' brushes.

5. **A. North America.** Most people don't know that camels originated in North America before humans were living on this continent. Scientists know they originated in North America be-cause they have found fossils of them. These ancient camels were much different from the ones that exist today. Some had long necks and looked like small giraffes, and others were small, about the size of a rabbit. These creatures spread out from North to South America where they became the llamas that live there today. Others crossed the land bridge that connected North America and Asia and became modern camels. Those that stayed in North America died out.

6. **A. It is carried around on a cart.** Fat-tail sheep were bred in far-eastern Asia. Their plump tails produce tallow, which is a white solid material that, when processed, can be used to make soap, candles, and lubricants. Eventually the sheep tails grew so fat that carts had to be hitched to the sheep to carry their tails around.

7. **B. Popcorn.** The binturong can be found in the tropical and sub-tropical forests of Southeast Asia. The scent, which smells like buttered popcorn, is believed to come from a gland located near the tail.

8. **A. Goat.** The Kashmir goat lives in mountainous regions of China and Iran and the Kashmir region of India.

9. **C. A relative of the cow.** Domesticated in India, China, and other places, a zebu is related to cows and oxen. It has short horns, thin legs, and a large hump over the shoulders. Some of the varieties are used as beasts of burden, while others are kept for milking or slaughtering. They are also used for riding. One member of this species is the Brahman, which Hindus regard as sacred.

10. **D. Brake.** The binturong lives in trees. It has black fur and can weigh up to 40 pounds. While the body of the binturong may be 39 inches long, the tail may add well over 20 inches more. It has a prehensile tail. This means that it can use its tail like a hand, similar to a monkey. It will wrap its tail around and grab a branch when climbing in the trees and hanging on branches. They are able to walk upside down, hanging from branches by using their tails. When running down a branch, the tail is also used as a brake. When a binturong rests in a tree, its tail holds onto the tree while it lies on its stomach.

11. **C. Perfume.** Taken from a pouch under the tails of civet cats, the civet scent is an important material used in the manufacturing of perfume. The scent is strong, but when it is diluted and used in small quantities, it gives a smoky aroma. The scent is also used in Africa to cure hair loss in women.

Name: _____ Date: _____

P E S W A S Y L M E R R

P · · · · · · · · · · · M
R · · · · · · · · · · · A
A · · · · · · · · · · · A
E · · · · · · · · · · · S
C · · · · · · · · · · · C
O · · · · · · · · · · · U
K · · · · · · · · · · · Y
N · · · · · · · · · · · E
A · · · · · · · · · · · D
C · · · · · · · · · · · H
N · · · · · · · · · · · E
E · · · · · · · · · · · T
I · · · · · · · · · · · T

U M S A E L D S B Y Y

Camel Puzzle

Bactrian Camel

Dromedary Camel

Humans domesticated camels many thousands of years ago, and they are still used today for milk, meat, and as beasts of burden in some parts of the world. There are two main species of camels. There is the Dromedary Camel, which has one hump, and the Bactrian Camel, which has two humps.

It is estimated that there are almost 13 million Dromedaries, almost all of them domesticated (not in the wild). However, Australia has about 700,000 feral camels that are descendants of camels that escaped in the nineteenth century. A feral animal is one that has escaped from domestication and has become wild. The Australian feral camel population is growing fast, and the government has decided to keep the population down by shooting them. They made this decision because the camels use too much of the resources needed by sheep farmers.

In some parts of Africa and Asia, camels still are used as they were in the past. They transport goods and people, and they pull plows. In Saudi Arabia, camels are still common, but they are not used as pack animals to any great extent. They are used as racing animals.

There is an interesting fact about camels hidden in the frame around the camel's picture shown above. To discover the fact, you must go around the frame twice, reading every *other* letter. Where do you start, and which way do you read around the frame? That's what you have to figure out.

Answer: _____

_____

21

Name: _____ Date: _____

Mammals: Elephants

Elephants, the largest living land animals, are sometimes called *pachyderms* from a Greek word which means "thick-skinned." The skin on an elephant's shoulder may be one and one-half inches thick. In addition to its skin, its huge size protects it from other animals. Its only enemies are humans. Elephants are usually peaceful creatures that live in family herds of 20–40 elephants of various ages. The herd is usually led by an old female called a cow. Elephants belong to an order called *Proboscidea*. There were once about 350 members of this order, but most have gradually became extinct. The two remaining members of this order are the African elephant and the Asian elephant. Asian elephants are more easily tamed. They do a lot of the hard work in India and Southeast Asia. They lift large trees between their tusks and trunk and drag them out of the forests.

Directions: Circle the letter of the correct answer(s).

1. Older female elephants are most valuable to the herd because:
   A. They give birth to multiple calves.
   C. Of their memory.
   B. They care for the young.
   D. They are good fighters.

2. An elephant is the only animal that has:
   A. Tusks.
   C. Trunks.
   B. Four knees.
   D. Large ears.

3. What is the largest of all animals?
   A. Giraffe
   C. Whale
   B. Elephant
   D. Rhinoceros

4. An elephant is pregnant for:
   A. 2 months.
   C. 22 months.
   B. 12 months.
   D. 42 months.

5. Elephants help the environment by:
   A. Building dams.
   C. Diverting streams.
   B. Planting tree seeds.
   D. Killing predators.

6. Elephants' greatest enemies are:
   A. Humans.
   C. Tigers.
   B. Lions.
   D. Tsetse flies.

Name: _____ Date: _____

Mammals: Elephants (cont.)

7. How many muscles are in an elephant's trunk?
    A. 100,000   B. 10,000
    C. 1,000   D. 100

8. Elephants greet each other by:
    A. Kissing.   B. Hugging.
    C. Trumpeting.   D. Dancing.

9. In order to comfort itself, a baby elephant may:
    A. Suck its trunk.   B. Sob.
    C. Carry a security leaf.   D. Adopt a mouse.

10. Elephants have:
    A. Weddings.   B. Funerals.
    C. Races.   D. Debates.

11. An elephant sends coded messages over short and long distances, which cannot be
    heard by humans. These messages are sent using:
    A. High-frequency sounds.   B. Low-frequency sounds.
    C. Quiet trumpeting.   D. Mental thoughts.

12. The elephant is the only mammal that can't:
    A. Nurse its young.   B. Lie down.
    C. Swim.   D. Jump.

13. A mother elephant calls to her young by:
    A. Trumpeting.   B. Slapping her ears against her head.
    C. Stomping.   D. Whistling.

14. From which of the following animals does ivory *not* come?
    A. Elephant   B. Walrus
    C. Elephant seal   D. Boar

15. In order to tell an African elephant from an Asian elephant, which part of the elephant is *not*
    helpful to study?
    A. Eyes   B. Feet
    C. Ears   D. Height

16. Which of the following is not a reason elephant babies take mudbaths?
    A. To keep cool   B. To keep away insects
    C. To disguise themselves   D. To avoid sunburn

Mammals: Elephants Answers

1. **C. Of their memory.** An older female elephant, called a cow, is important to her family's survival because of her memory. Over the years, the older cows have visited all parts of their range many times. Because of this experience, the cow is able to remember where food and water will be during various seasons. During a drought, for example, she may remember the location of a dried-up lake where water can be found by digging just below the surface. This is important because an adult elephant must have at least fifteen gallons of water each day in order to survive. The older female is also able to steer her family away from dangerous areas.

2. **B. Four knees.** The elephant seal also has a trunk or **proboscis,** which the male, or bull, uses to amplify its calls. The elephant seal is a large animal that can weigh up to four tons. Their size and their trunks are the reasons they are called elephant seals. Other animals also have tusks.

3. **C. Whale.** The blue whale is the largest of all animals, while the elephant is the largest animal that lives on land.

4. **C. 22 months.** That's almost two years.

5. **B. Planting tree seeds.** Because of their size and enormous appetite, elephants have a great impact on their environment. They destroy many trees as they feed. On the other hand, they are responsible for planting trees. The acacia tree in Africa has tasty seedpods that elephants love. While the pods are digested in their stomachs, the seeds are very tough and travel unharmed through the elephant's digestive system. Eventually, the seeds pass out of the elephant with the elephant's dung. The dung is rich in nutrients, and within a short time, new trees begin to grow.

6. **A. Humans.** Because of their thick skin and their size, adult African elephants have no enemies, except for humans. Elephants are hunted for their ivory tusks. In 1980, there were about 1.2 million elephants in Africa. By 1990, illegal hunters, called poachers, had reduced the elephant population to about 625,000. In the latter part of 1989, there was a world-wide ban on ivory when the Convention on International Trade in Endangered Species put the elephant on its most-endangered species list. Seventy-five nations support this ban by not allowing illegally obtained ivory to be imported into their countries. In addition to poaching, the destruction of its African habitat threatens elephants.

7. **A. 100,000.** An elephant's trunk is amazing. With 100,000 muscles, it is strong enough to carry a tree, but can also pick up a leaf. The muscles allow it to bend and grasp much like an arm and hand. The trunk can be used to pick up water for a shower or to spray into the elephant's mouth. It can pick fruit off of a tree or spray dust to keep down parasites.

8. **B. Hugging.** Elephants are friendly, social creatures that use their trunks to show affection and comfort. When they greet each other or want to show affection, they sometimes hug by wrapping their trunks together.

9. **A. Suck its trunk.** Just as a human child may suck its thumb, an elephant baby (calf) may suck its trunk for comfort.

10. **B. Funerals.** It has long been believed that elephants can live up to 150 years, but there is no actual proof or record of any elephant reaching this age. In captivity, an elephant usually lives about 70 years. It is a long-held belief that there are elephant graveyards where elephants go to die. No evidence of this has ever been found. Perhaps this story began when groups of

Mammals: Elephants Answers (cont.)

dead elephants have been found in one location. It is now believed that these animals may have been killed at the same time by some catastrophe. Maybe poachers killed a group for their ivory. Or perhaps a group may have died of thirst or as a result of a fire. But elephants do seem to understand death to some degree. Except for humans, elephants are the only other animal that shows fear when they find the bones of their own kind. Elephants grieve at the loss of a relative, friend, or stillborn baby. There have even been records of elephants burying their dead. Once in Sudan, a hunter killed an elephant, and when he came back the next day, he found the elephant's body had been buried eighteen inches beneath the soil. A close examination showed evidence that the grave had been dug with elephant tusks.

11. **B. Low-frequency sounds.** An elephant uses a secret code of low-frequency sounds in order to communicate. The low-frequency sounds are very loud, but because they are of such a low frequency, humans are unable to hear them. However, elephants are able to hear these low-frequency sounds at more than five miles away.

12. **D. Jump.**

13. **B. Slapping her ears against her head.**

14. **C. Elephant seal.**

15. **A. Eyes.** The Asian and African elephants are similar, but a close examination reveals their obvious differences. The Asian elephant is smaller, its ears are smaller, and the females do not have tusks. On the front feet, the Asian has five nails compared to the African's four and on the back feet, the Asian has four nails as compared to the African's three. The Asian has a smoother trunk and one little tip at the end of it, and the African has two tips at the end of its trunk. The Asian's back humps up, while the African's slopes down.

16. **C. To disguise themselves.** A baby elephant takes mudbaths for many reasons: to protect itself from sunburn, to keep cool, and to get rid of insects. Adult elephants also roll around in the mud or pick the mud up with their trunks and throw it so it lands on their bodies.

African Elephant

Asian Elephant

Name: _____ Date: _____

Amazing Mammals Fact Puzzle

Directions: Using the grid on the following page and the clues below, learn an interesting fact about a mammal. Some of the instructions will direct you to "write" a specific letter, rather than using the grid.

1. Pick the letter that is between the letters V and Z.
2. Pick the letter that is at the very bottom and the farthest to the right.
3. Pick the letter that is the farthest away from the last letter.
4. Pick the letter under R and over J.
5. Pick the letter between C and S.
6. Pick the letter that has its twin above it and a Q to its right.
7. Pick the letter in the basement the farthest to the left.
8. Pick the letter that is one level above and one box to the right of the Q and one level below and one box to the left of the F.
9. Pick the letter on the grid that is located before the first letter of the alphabet and behind the eighth.
10. Pick the letter on the grid that is located above the last letter of the alphabet and below the eighteenth.
11. *Write* the first letter of a two-letter word that spells an animal of the bovine family.
12. Pick the letter surrounded by Q, U, B, and T.
13. Pick the letter that does not have another letter above it or to its left.
14. Pick the letter that is diagonal between two U's.
15. Pick the letter above V and below W.
16. *Write* the letter that is the middle letter of a three-letter name for a flightless bird found in Australia.
17. *Write* the first letter of a three-letter name for an electrical fish.
18. Pick the letter that has an R to its left and nothing to its right.
19. Pick the letter between Y and F.
20. Pick the letter that has no letter below it and only one letter to its right.
21. Pick the letter between two F's.
22. Pick the letter between two K's.
23. *Write* the letter that if it were a number, it would have no value.
24. *Write* the letter that is the middle letter of a three-letter abbreviation of the word *professional*.
25. Pick the letter between W and R.
26. Pick the only letter that has its twin above it and a V to its right.
27. Pick the letter that has O and U immediately above it and O and A immediately below it.
28. Pick the letter that is the skinniest.
29. Pick the letter that is the farthest to the left and the farthest down on the grid.
30. Pick the letter that has a J above it and no letter below it.

Name: _____ Date: _____

Amazing Mammals Fact Puzzle (cont.)

Directions: Using the clues on the previous page and the grid below, learn an interesting fact about a mammal. Some of the instructions will direct you to "write" a specific letter, rather than using the grid.

E	M	U	Q	L	K	N	K	X	C
H	I	H	T	Y	G	F	L	P	D
I	V	E	Z	U	Q	A	F	J	R
D	W	B	X	O	E	T	S	R	S
M	A	E	D	L	Q	K	U	P	Y
J	Z	P	R	O	X	C	V	J	W
V	C	H	S	A	T	B	G	E	I
W	K	R	Y	A	Q	M	T	E	V
B	F	S	F	H	J	U	D	L	X
N	B	Z	Y	U	G	I	P	O	L

Answer: __ __ __ __ __ __ __ __

__ __ __ __ __ __ __ __ __ __   __ __

__ __ __ __ __ __ __ __ __

Name: _____ Date: _____

Mammals: Hippopotamus and Rhinoceros

There are five species of rhinoceros. The two African rhinos are the white and black rhinos, and there are three Asian species. The five species range in weight from 750 pounds to 8,000 pounds and are four-and-a-half to six-feet tall.

The hippopotamus is a plant-eating, water-loving animal. Hippos are relatives of pigs, camels, and deer. The center of a hippo's life during the day is water. It plays, fights, mates, and even gives birth in the water. At night, the hippo comes out of the water to graze on land.

Directions: Circle the letter of the correct answer(s).

1. A rhinoceros horn is made of:
    A. Bone.   B. Gristle.   C. Hair.   D. Skin.

2. A rhino's nostrils are:
    A. Bigger than their brains.   B. The home for small worms.
    C. Used to communicate.   D. A weapon.

3. The word *hippopotamus* comes from two Greek words that mean:
    A. Fat dancer.   B. River pig.   C. River horse.   D. Water bear.

4. A white rhinoceros is _____ and a black rhinoceros is _____.
    A. white, black   B. black, white
    C. gray, black   D. gray, gray

5. Except for the whale, which animal has the largest mouth?
    A. Elephant   B. Rhinoceros   C. Hippopotamus   D. Alligator

6. George Washington's false teeth were made of:
    A. Wood.   B. Rhinoceros horn.
    C. Hippopotamus tusk.   D. Donkey bones.

7. For the first year of their lives, young hippos nurse:
    A. On land.   B. Under water.
    C. Either under water or on land.   D. Only with the father present.

8. The main reason people poach (illegally hunt) rhinos is for their:
    A. Meat.   B. Tusks.   C. Horns.   D. Hides.

9. Which animal is responsible for more deaths in the wild?
    A. Hippopotamus   B. Rhinoceros   C. Lions   D. Crocodiles

10. A group of rhinos is called a:
    A. Coalition.   B. Mob.   C. Bunch.   D. Crash.

Mammals: Hippopotamus and Rhinoceros Answers

1. **C. Hair.** Unlike antelope horns, rhinoceros horns are not composed of bone and do not have any bone in them. They are made of keratin, which is the main ingredient of hair, fingernails, and hoofs. The hair-like fibers are so strong and packed together that the rhino's horn is a dangerous weapon.

2. **A. Bigger than their brains.** They have a highly developed sense of smell.

3. **C. River horse.** In fact, hippos are related more closely to pigs than to horses. People often say that hippos sweat blood. While it appears that they do, what they actually sweat is an oily, red pigment that lubricates and protects their skin.

4. **D. Gray, gray.** The white rhino has about the same color skin as the black rhino. Both are gray. Their names probably came from the color of the dirt that covered their bodies.

5. **C. Hippopotamus.** Next to the elephant, the hippo is the heaviest of all land mammals and can weigh 8,000 pounds. When its mouth is completely open, the opening measures four feet. A hippo's stomach is 10 feet long and can hold six bushels of grass.

6. **C. Hippopotamus tusk**. Many people think that George Washington's teeth were made from wood. This isn't true. Washington had gradually lost his teeth at a young age, and by the time he was inaugurated president, he had only one tooth left. Over his lifetime, Washington had dentures made from all sorts of materials, such as ivory, gold, lead, human teeth, and animal teeth. But the false teeth he used the longest and most successfully were made from hippopotamus ivory and gold. Hippopotamus ivory was a better material for false teeth than elephant ivory because it did not turn yellow as it got older. But the materials from which the upper and lower dental plates were made is not the whole story. These dental plates were held into place with springs that pushed them against the roof of his mouth and the bottom of his mouth. Washington had to exert pressure together in order to close his jaws together, otherwise his mouth would pop open. Historians believe that this is the reason that the president looks so serious in his portraits. In addition, these false teeth were just a bit large for his mouth, which gave Washington a strange expression.

7. **C. Either under water or on land.** For the first year of their life, the youngsters nurse either under water or on land, depending on where mom is when they get hungry. After they're weaned, calves remain with their mothers until fully grown, at about eight years of age.

8. **C. Horns.** People of some cultures believe that rhino horn can cure certain diseases. In spite of the fact it has never been proved that a rhino horn has any medical benefits, it is the main reason for poaching the species. In order to protect the rhino, many things have been tried. There have been programs to educate people that rhino horns do not have health benefits. There have been increased patrols by rangers, a dehorning program for rhinos, and the relocation of rhinos to safer areas. Some countries have even developed a policy to shoot poachers on sight.

9. **A. Hippopotamus.** If you don't count the mosquito, many experts say that the hippo is Africa's most dangerous animal and kills more humans. Hippos have killed many more people than rhinos, lions, or crocodiles. Some rogue tigers have killed a lot of people too, but tigers live in India, not Africa. The hippos are not only aggressive animals, but they do not fear humans. They will tip a boat over and kill those on it with a few quick bites. Most deaths happen when a person gets between the hippo and deep water or between a mother and her calf.

10. **D. Crash.**

Name: _____ Date: _____

Mammals: Giraffes

Giraffes live in herds in Africa south of the Sahara. The giraffe is the tallest of all mammals, reaching a height of 18 feet. While its body is not unusually large, its legs and neck are very long. Both sexes have two to four short horns. Their legs and necks are so long that in order to get a drink, they must bend and spread their front legs. Most of a giraffe's diet consists of leaves from the acacia tree. Giraffes are plentiful in east Africa because they are protected. But in other parts of Africa, the number of giraffes has been lowered by hunters. In the past, Arabs considered the giraffe a gift of peace and friendship. It is likely that they chose a giraffe because it is a very gentle creature.

Directions: Circle the letters of the correct answer(s).

1. When Europeans first saw a giraffe, they called it a:
    A. Cameleopard.
    B. Longnecker.
    C. Spotted horse.
    D. Roscoe.

2. A giraffe's tongue can be:
    A. 6 inches long.
    B. 11 inches long.
    C. 21 inches long.
    D. 36 inches long.

3. A newborn giraffe is about:
    A. The size of a peanut.
    B. Six inches long.
    C. Six feet tall.
    D. 300 pounds.

4. The giraffe usually sleeps:
    A. Standing up.
    B. In water.
    C. Once a week.
    D. 36 hours at a time.

5. Giraffes can go weeks without:
    A. Eating.
    B. Drinking.
    C. Sleeping.
    D. Seeing another giraffe.

6. When giraffes fight, they fight by:
    A. Biting.
    B. Butting.
    C. Kicking.
    D. Swinging their necks back and forth.

7. Adult giraffes usually drink or rest in:
    A. Nests.
    B. Lakes.
    C. Shifts.
    D. Groups of three.

8. Which has the most neck bones?
    A. Humans.
    B. Giraffes.
    C. Mice.
    D. Whales.

9. A giraffe is capable of growing at a rate of:
    A. One-half inch per month.
    B. One-half inch per week.
    C. One-half inch per day.
    D. One-half inch per hour.

Mammals: Giraffes Answers

1. **A. Cameleopard.** They assumed the giraffe was a cross between a camel and a leopard. However, Africans had always known about and honored giraffes. Prehistoric man drew pictures of them on the walls of caves. Ancient Egyptians used giraffes in paintings and designs. The hides are still used for ceremonial shields, and the tail hairs are used for jewelry.

2. **C. 21 inches long.** A giraffe is capable of using its tongue to clean its ears. A giraffe's tongue is also prehensile, which means it can grab and hold onto objects. The tongue is not the only part of the giraffe that is large. A giraffe's heart is 2 feet long and weighs 24 pounds.

3. **C. Six feet tall.** A newborn giraffe is about 6 feet (1.9 meters) tall at birth and weighs about 150 pounds. When most animals are born, the mother lies down so that the newborn comes into the world with little stress. This is not the case with giraffes. The mother giraffe stands while giving birth, and the newborn falls six feet to the ground and lands on its head.

   Baby giraffes live in a very dangerous world. Lions and other animals like eating them, so the babies must learn to walk quickly. A baby giraffe can walk within 20 minutes of birth and can usually run with the herd the next day. It learns to run fast and to stay on its feet. Many calves are eaten by lions during their first year of life. Once a giraffe becomes an adult, however, its height is often enough to protect it from lions. A giraffe's neck is six feet long and weighs about 600 pounds. Its legs are also six feet long. While the back legs look shorter than the front legs, they are actually about the same length. Their powerful front legs with sharp hooves can kill an attacking lion. Once grown, giraffes can easily live 25 years.

4. **A. Standing up.** The giraffe usually sleeps standing up, because it can take too long for it to get back up on its feet if a predator should approach it.

5. **B. Drinking.** Giraffes can go weeks without drinking water. They can go even longer without water than camels can. When they do drink, they can drink up to 10 gallons at a time. Giraffes can get most of the water they need from the plants they eat.

6. **D. Swinging their necks back and forth.** Adult male giraffes bang their long necks together in a form of ritual fighting, during which no harm is done to either giraffe. They each try to hit their opponent between the shoulder and the ear.

7. **C. Shifts.** Adult giraffes must be careful of lions when they are bending down to drink water or to rest. Because of this, they usually drink or rest in shifts so that at least one giraffe is always on the lookout for approaching predators.

8. **All have the same number.** Giraffes, humans, whales, and mice all have the same number of bones in their necks. A giraffe's neck bones are just much longer!

9. **D. One-half inch per hour.** A London zoo reported that a baby giraffe measured five feet, two inches shortly after birth. A day later it was six feet, three inches tall.

Name: _____ Date: _____

Mammals: Old World Monkeys

Monkeys are generally classified into two groups. There are New World monkeys and Old World monkeys. New World monkeys live in Central and South America. Old World monkeys are found in Africa and Asia and on several islands. Old World monkeys are more varied than those in the New World. Some Old World monkeys spend most of their time in treetops, but others live both in the trees and on the ground. Those who live on the ground generally eat insects, small animals, and plants, while those who live in the trees only eat leaves and fruit. The monkeys who live both on the ground and in the trees are generally more intelligent than those who live in the trees all of the time.

Directions: Circle the letter of the correct answer(s).

1. When a low-ranking rhesus monkey is with a high-ranking monkey, in order to avoid aggression, the low-ranking rhesus monkey will:
   A.   Bow.   B.   Cry.   C.   Pretend to be stupid.   D.   Run away.

2. The velvet monkeys of Africa have a(n) _____ that some consider the closest animal _____ to that of humans. (Put the same word in each blank.)
   A.   Intelligence   B.   Language   C.   Family   D.   Diet

3. A baboon will scare off a rival by:
   A.   Screaming and gesturing.   B.   Dancing and singing.
   C.   Blinking and yawning.   D.   Acting hurt and retreating.

4. A male Barbary macaque enjoys nothing more than:
   A.   Making baskets.   B.   Braiding its hair.
   C.   Planting trees.   D.   Babysitting.

5. The Japanese macaque has one great pleasure in life:
   A.   Taking a hot bath during a snowstorm.   B.   Drinking white wine.
   C.   Diving.   D.   Eating strawberries.

6. One of the strangest-looking monkeys is the proboscis monkey. It is a strange-looking monkey because of its:
   A.   Colorful face.   B.   Long hair.   C.   Pointed ears.   D.   Big nose.

7. Only African and Asian monkeys can:
   A.   Swing from their tails.   B.   Use tools.
   C.   Eat meat.   D.   See reds and greens.

8. The patas monkey is sometimes called the:
   A.   Military monkey.   B.   Organ grinder's monkey.
   C.   Monkey Khan.   D.   Lucky monkey.

Name: _____ Date: _____

Mammals: Old World Monkeys (cont.)

9. When a silvered leaf monkey, which is native to Borneo, is born, it is:
   A. Hairless.   B. Pink.
   C. Striped.   D. Bright orange.

10. Celebes macaques are short-tailed lowland macaques that:
    A. Have their own hairdressers.   B. Prefer eating crocodile eggs.
    C. Fish for crabs.   D. Go on vacations.

11. Pig-tailed macaques are trained by Malays to:
    A. Keep house.   B. Pick ripe coconuts.
    C. Babysit.   D. Hunt.

12. It is recorded that the Egyptians trained baboons to:
    A. Fight.   B. Help build the pyramids.
    C. Wait on tables.   D. Act as sentries.

13. Young rhesus macaques spend much of their day playing. Their playing consists of chasing, wrestling, and pretend fighting. In order for one rhesus macaque to signal another that it intends to play and not really fight, it will look at its opponent:
    A. With a smile.   B. With fingers crossed.
    C. And then look down.   D. Upside down and through its own legs.

14. The Barbary macaque is a type of monkey. When one male is threatened by another male, the first macaque immediately:
    A. Runs away.   B. Shows the other male his baby.
    C. Acts like a clown.   D. Pretends to be injured.

15. In Ancient Egypt, Hamadryas baboons were believed to be:
    A. Men who had been cursed.   B. Oracles of the god Thoth.
    C. Persians.   D. Devil's disciples.

16. Each morning in the southeast as dawn breaks, a male and female gibbon will:
    A. Begin to dance.   B. Sing a duet.
    C. Wash their young.   D. Walk the perimeter of their territory.

17. There are usually about 70 baboons in a family unit, which is headed by a dominant male that is:
    A. Tall.   B. Small.
    C. Fat.   D. Skinny.

Mammals: Old World Monkeys Answers

1. **C. Pretend to be stupid.** Low-ranking rhesus monkeys, which live in Asia, pretend to be stupid in order to avoid conflict with dominant monkeys. In tests that involved both low-ranking rhesus monkeys and dominant monkeys, the dominant monkeys learned new tasks quickly, while lower-ranking monkeys took much longer. Additional tests revealed a startling fact. When the lower-ranking monkeys were taught new tasks without a dominant monkey present, they learned just as quickly as the dominant monkeys did. The researchers concluded that while having a dominant monkey present did not prevent the low-ranking members from learning, it did prevent them from revealing what they learned. The low-rankers preferred to "play dumb" rather than to risk being attacked by the dominant monkey.

2. **B. Language.** They have "words" or sounds that indicate to the rest of their group the identity of a specific danger. For example, there is a specific sound for warning the group that there is a snake closeby, another sound warns of a leopard, and still another will tell the group that there is a bird of prey around. Not only do the "words" describe the kind of danger, they also tell where the danger is. If the danger is down below, a monkey shouts a warning, and the rest of the group will look down and immediately climb up the trees. If the danger is from above, such as a bird of prey, a specific warning tells the monkeys to quickly go down the trees and hide under brush.

3. **C. Blinking and yawning.** Dominance in a troop is important since those who are most dominant have the first choice of food and mating partners. When trying to assert his dominance, a baboon will first stare at his rival, then raise his eyebrows and retract his scalp in order to show his colored eyelids. If that doesn't work, he will then blink very quickly and rapidly. He will next show his teeth by yawning. If none of these actions work, he will fight.

4. **D. Babysitting.** Barbary macaque monkeys live in groups of 10–30 and are found in Algeria, Gibraltar, Morocco, and Tunisia. The male macaque plays an important role in raising the young. He will not only babysit for his own offspring, he may find another young macaque that he likes and carry him around with him. He will play with the young monkey, groom him, and show him off to others in the group. When a female Barbary macaque looks for a mate, she will often look for a male she thinks will be a good parent.

5. **A. Taking a hot bath during a snowstorm.** Japanese macaques are large, muscular, shaggy-haired monkeys with short, furry tails and pink faces. They live farther north than any other monkeys or apes. On Honshu island, which is the largest of the four main islands of Japan, there are steaming spring waters that stay warm all winter, and a group of macaques will relax during a blizzard in the hot water. Macaques were important in Japanese myths and folk tales. If you have ever seen the Buddhist monkeys that represent the saying, "see no evil, hear no evil, speak no evil," you have seen a picture of a Japanese macaque. With the exception of humans, macaques are the most widespread group of primates.

6. **D. Big nose.** Proboscis means "nose." While both male and females have large, fat noses, the male's is larger. It is so long, in fact, that it might hang down right over its mouth, so that he needs to push it up and out of the way when he eats. When he tilts his head back to look up, the nose flops back and hits him between the eyes. The male's nose swells and becomes red when the monkey is excited or angry. When he senses danger or wants to attract a female, he uses his nose to make loud "honks." This honking straightens his flexible nose. The proboscis monkey is a vegetarian that lives in groups of about 20. The young have

Mammals: Old World Monkeys Answers (cont.)

blue faces. The proboscis monkey likes to swim. It sometimes dives into the water from trees that are 50 feet above the water.

7. **D. See reds and greens.** While most mammals are able to see yellows and blues, only African and Asian monkeys can also see reds and greens. South American monkeys are color-blind. Being able to see the colors red and green is important because it helps monkeys find ripening fruit.

8. **A. Military monkey.** The patas monkey has a red coat and appears to have a mustache that makes him look like a nineteenth-century army colonel. The patas monkey lives in groups with one male leader and twenty females. It is the leader's job to protect the group from danger. He protects them by keeping a lookout for predators, and if he spots one coming towards the group, he makes noises and leads the predators away from the group. In other words, he acts as a decoy to save his family. He is able to do this because he can run 35 miles per hour. The patas monkey is also called the dancing red monkey or the Hussar monkey.

9. **D. Bright orange.** Adults have dark fur. When a baby is born, every female in the group inspects and grooms the baby. When the mother goes looking for food, the babies are cared for by a babysitter.

10. **C. Fish for crabs.** Crab-eating macaques are long-tailed monkeys with brown faces. They fish for crabs and other crustaceans.

11. **B. Pick ripe coconuts.**

12. **C. Wait on tables.** The Egyptians trained baboons to perform many duties.

13. **D. Upside down and through its own legs.** Playing is not just an amusement for a young macaque. It teaches it some very basic lessons. Playing teaches it fighting and wrestling skills and also teaches it how far it can go in play without hurting another. Probably the most important reason for the play is that it shows the young macaques which in their troop is the strongest and best fighter. This will help determine the pecking order, or social status, within their troop.

14. **B. Shows the other male his baby.** The males do not like to fight, and if another male acts unfriendly, it shows that male his baby. The other male then forgets the threats and fusses over the baby.

15. **B. Oracles of the god Thoth.** It was believed that Thoth, the ancient Egyptian god of learning, had Hamadryas baboons as companions and oracles. The baboons were given the honor of being mummified when they died. Many mummified bodies of these baboons have been unearthed. The Hamadryas baboons were also trained by the Egyptians to perform many duties.

16. **B. Sing a duet.** This duet can be heard up to two miles away. As the male and female sing, they may swing from branch to branch displaying graceful movements. It is thought that the purpose of this duet is to announce to all that can hear that these two Gibbons claim this territory for their own.

17. **B. Small.** Being small makes it easier for the male to build his harem because he kidnaps young females from their mothers in order to add to his family. A small male is able to move swiftly without getting caught.

Name: _____ Date: _____

Odd Mammal Fact From History

Directions: On the following page are a number of descriptions of mammals. Fill in the spaces below with the correct animal that goes with the description. Then take the letters in the circles and put them in the spaces below the puzzle. The words that are spelled from these letters tell you what happened to some animals during the Middle Ages.

1.
2.
3.
4.
5.
6.
7.
8.
9.
10.
11.
12.
13.
14.
15.
16.
17.
18.
19.

ANSWER: __ __ __ __   __ __   __ __ __ __ __   __ __ __   __ __ __ __ __ __

Name: _____ Date: _____

Odd Mammal Fact From History (cont.)

1. This is a horned mammal with two-toed hooves and smooth brown or gray hair. Some of the better-known kinds of these animals are impalas, gazelles, and gnus.
2. This is a small rodent with a long bushy tail that lives in trees and eats nuts.
3. This is the largest member of the cat family, with a sandy-colored coat and black stripes.
4. A large African or Asian monkey that lives on the ground, it has large teeth and a protruding snout.
5. This is an Australian marsupial.
6. A member of the weasel family, this carnivore lives near water and eats fish, birds, frogs and other small animals. Its head is flat and has short, rounded ears. Its webbed feet have claws. There is one variety that lives in rivers and another that lives in the ocean.
7. Found in Africa, this member of the horse family can be identified by its black-and-white stripes.
8. This large member of the cat family is sometimes referred to as the king of beasts.
9. This is the tallest mammal that can be identified by its exceptionally long neck.
10. This is the name for the many different kinds of small antelopes; the animals are very fast and are good jumpers.
11. This is a bear found in China. Instead of being colored a shade of black or brown, this animal is mainly white but has black patches over its legs, eyes and ears. It lives in the mountains and mainly eats bamboo.
12. This is a highly intelligent primate that has grasping hands and forward-facing eyes; many have prehensile tails, which means that their tails can grab and hold onto something, like a limb.
13. This is a burrowing mammal from Africa; it has a long snout, strong claws, heavy tail, and a tongue that extends to eat ants and termites. It is sometimes confused with the South American anteater.
14. This animal is the largest land animal. It has long, curved tusks made of ivory. It also has a long snout that it uses to pick up things.
15. This small, furry mammal has long ears, a short tail, large front teeth, and large hind legs that make it good at running and jumping. This rodent is found in many suburban yards or found nibbling in a vegetable garden.
16. This mammal is sometimes called a sea cow because it grazes on water grasses and plants. Its numbers have been reduced by hunters and collisions with boats. Ancient sailors thought these animals were mermaids.
17. This is a wild dog found in Australia.
18. This is a large mammal that is used in the deserts of Asia and northern Africa. The one or two humps on its back store fat. It can go three weeks without water.
19. Covered by a layer of bony plates that protects it from enemies, this animal is found in the southern part of the United States, as well as in South and Central America. It is related to the sloth and the anteater.

37

Name: _____ Date: _____

Mammals: New World Monkeys

Monkeys are generally classified into two groups. There are Old World monkeys and New World monkeys. Old World monkeys are found in Africa and Asia and several islands. Old World monkeys are more varied than those in the New World. Some Old World monkeys spend most of their time in treetops, but others live both in the trees and on the ground. Those who live on the ground generally eat insects, small animals and plants, while those who live in the trees only eat leaves and fruit. The monkeys who live both on the ground and in the trees are generally smarter than those who live in the trees all of the time.

New World monkeys live in Central and South America. They are tree-dweller monkeys, such as spider monkeys, howler monkeys, and woolly monkeys. They have prehensile tails that they can wrap around branches and use like an extra arm or leg. A monkey that has a prehensile tail is able to hold itself up by its tail alone as it swings back and forth and gathers fruit.

Directions: Circle the letter of the correct answer(s).

1. A Capuchin monkey is named after:
   A.   A Franciscan monk.
   B.   The scientist who discovered it.
   C.   The sound it makes.
   D.   The forest where it lives.

2. A Capuchin monkey is sometimes called:
   A.   A spider monkey.
   B.   Kenny.
   C.   An organ grinder's monkey.
   D.   A circus monkey.

3. In a marmoset family, who cares for the young?
   A.   Father   B.   Mother   C.   Grandmother   D.   Brothers and sisters

4. One of the strangest New World monkeys is the owl monkey. It is the only monkey that:
   A.   Sleeps during the day.
   B.   Has a call that sounds like "Who."
   C.   Sees in the dark.
   D.   Has large eyes.

5. Monkeys are important in:
   A.   Growing passion fruit.
   B.   Keeping snakes out of the forest.
   C.   Pollinating flowers.
   D.   Grooming gorillas.

6. The male howler monkey of Central and South America establishes its territory by:
   A.   Fighting.
   B.   Spreading its scent.
   C.   Loud arguments.
   D.   Breaking branches.

7. Which of the following is *not* a reason that monkeys groom each other?
   A.   To show social status   B.   To communicate   C.   To discipline   D.   To clean

8. When the female cotton-topped tamarin gives birth, the male:
   A.   Leaves and never returns.
   B.   Helps deliver the baby.
   C.   Sings a song.
   D.   Seeks a new mate.

Mammals: New World Monkeys Answers

1. **A. A Franciscan monk**. Capuchin monkeys are considered among the most intelligent monkeys in the New World. The name comes from the black fur on the top of its head that resembles a Franciscan monk's cowl, or hood, which is called a capuche. Capuchins enjoy a varied diet. They feed on fruit, vegetation, and small animals. While they feed on over 95 plant species, palm fruits are preferred.

2. **C. An organ grinder's monkey.** Many years ago, even as late as the early part of the twentieth century, capuchin monkeys would travel with a man called an organ grinder. The man had a barrel organ. A barrel organ was a small organ-like musical instrument that could be carried or rolled on a small cart. The organ grinder would dress a capuchin monkey in clothes and tie it to the organ. The organ grinder would play the organ, and when people would gather around, the monkey would go around the crowd and beg for coins.

3. **A. Father.** In a marmoset family, the father cares for the young and carries them about. The mother usually carries her young only when she is nursing them. Marmosets usually have twins, who are not identical, so one could be a male, and the other a female.

4. **A. Sleeps during the day.** The owl monkey is the only **nocturnal** monkey. It sleeps during the day, and at night it comes out to feed on fruit, insects, and leaves. At night, the male will hoot in order to find his female and to proclaim his territory. The owl monkey mates for life, and the father takes care of the children.

5. **A. Growing passion fruit.** Passion fruit is a fruit that is available in the rain forest, and monkeys love to eat it. After the seeds pass through their bodies and fall onto the ground, new passion fruit trees will grow. Also, seeds of the African baobab tree sprout more easily if they are first eaten by a baboon and then passed through its digestive tract. Apparently, the baboon's digestive juices erode the seed coat, permitting water to penetrate the seed more readily.

6. **C. Loud arguments.** Howlers live in groups within territories whose boundaries are mapped out by "arguments," called howling matches, with neighboring troops. While both the male and female are able to howl, it is the male howler that is the loudest. Howling lets other monkeys know they are around. Often, other howler monkeys will answer back, and there will be a long howling battle between the two groups. This avoids physical conflict between the two groups.

   There are several species of howlers that are found throughout Central and South America. Howlers are the largest New World monkeys and reach lengths of 28 inches, not counting the tail. Howlers are bearded and have a hunched appearance. They have a prehensile tail. Their voices carry anywhere from two to three miles and are heard at dusk, dawn, and during rainstorms. Some people have claimed that they have heard howlers that were ten miles away.

7. **C. To discipline.** Monkeys groom to keep clean as well as to indicate a social status. A monkey will groom those of a higher social status. Grooming is a social act that keeps the group of monkeys together. Touching while grooming is also a form of communication.

8. **B. Helps deliver the baby.** The female usually gives birth to twins. The father helps with the birth and then washes the newborns. The father carries the young, but gives them back to the mother when it is feeding time.

Name: _____ Date: _____

What's the Difference?

Directions: On the lines below, explain in your own words the difference between each of the pairs of animals listed. Continue on your own paper, if necessary.

1. Rabbit—Hare _____

    _____

    _____

    _____

2. Bactrian Camel—Dromedary Camel

    _____

    _____

    _____

3. Moose—Elk _____

    _____

    _____

    _____

4. Caribou—Reindeer _____

    _____

    _____

    _____

5. Bat—Bird _____

    _____

    _____

    _____

6. Porpoise—Dolphin _____

    _____

    _____

    _____

7. Rat—Mouse _____

    _____

    _____

    _____

8. Buffalo—Bison _____

    _____

    _____

    _____

9. Weasel—Ermine _____

    _____

    _____

    _____

10. Manatee—Dugong _____

    _____

    _____

    _____

11. Seal—Sea Lion _____

    _____

    _____

    _____

Name: _____ Date: _____

Mammals: Chimpanzees

Apes and monkeys are sometimes confused with each other. They are both primates, and though they appear to be similar, a close examination will show that apes do not have tails, and their arms are usually longer than their legs. Zoologists divide apes into two families: the lesser apes, or gibbons, and the great apes. The great apes include the gorilla, the orangutan, and two kinds of chimpanzee. Apes live in tropical woodlands and the forests of Africa and Asia.

Chimpanzees are a species of ape that, along with the bonobo, is more closely related to humans than any other animal. Chimpanzees live in the tropical forests and savannas of equatorial Africa. While individual chimpanzees vary in size and appearance, most are between 3–5.5 feet tall when standing erect and weigh between 70–130 pounds. Males tend to be larger and more robust than females. Their skin is white, but the face, hands, and feet are black. Younger animals can be pink or white. Chimpanzees have brown or black hair with bare faces, except for a short white beard. A chimpanzee can use its foot like a hand. It has an opposable big toe that is used like a thumb. That is what enables a chimp to hold onto a branch of a tree with its foot and dangle. As chimpanzees age, both the males and females become bald on their foreheads, and their backs become gray.

Directions: Circle the letter of the correct answer(s).

1. The chimpanzee usually warns others that a predator is nearby by:
   A.   Grinning.
   B.   Shrieking.
   C.   Hand gestures.
   D.   Waving a branch.

2. Which of the following is not a threatening gesture among chimpanzees?
   A.   Showing teeth
   B.   A clenched fist
   C.   Staring
   D.   Slapping the ground

3. It is apparent that two chimps are playing and not fighting:
   A.   If they are not making sounds.
   B.   If they are "chattering."
   C.   If they have on their "play faces."
   D.   If other chimps are not observing them.

4. When a chimp in the wild becomes ill, he
   A.   Is killed.
   B.   Is avoided.
   C.   Takes medicine.
   D.   Is treated by the oldest female.

5. When chimpanzees meet, which of the following behaviors would *not* occur?
   A.   Kiss
   B.   Hug
   C.   Grin
   D.   Shake hands and bow

6. Most people do not realize that chimpanzees sometimes:
   A.   Swim.
   B.   Plant yams.
   C.   Fish.
   D.   Hunt.

Name: _____ Date: _____

Mammals: Chimpanzees (cont.)

7. Chimpanzees are one of the few animals that:
   - A. Grow vegetables.
   - B. Use tools.
   - C. Eat both meat and vegetables.
   - D. Fish.

8. Which of the following games do young chimps *not* play?
   - A. Duck, Duck, Mongoose
   - B. Hide and seek
   - C. Wrestling
   - D. Peekaboo

9. Chimps build a nest by weaving branches in a tree each night. Approximately how long does it take them to do this?
   - A. A minute
   - B. Ten minutes
   - C. Thirty minutes
   - D. An hour

10. When a chimpanzee becomes old, it:
    - A. Is killed.
    - B. Is treated well.
    - C. Is sent away.
    - D. Voluntarily leaves the troop.

11. In April 2005, a South African zoo tried to persuade its star chimpanzee to:
    - A. Stop smoking.
    - B. Eat vegetables.
    - C. Stop singing.
    - D. Not squirt spectators with a garden hose

Mammals: Chimpanzees Answers

1. **A. Grinning.** The chimpanzee usually warns others that danger is nearby, not by screaming, but by its expression. When danger in the form of a predator is near, the chimp will give a fear grin that will alert the other chimps of danger. Why not a loud shriek that may alert the others more quickly? While shrieking or screaming is sometimes used, it is not the preferred method of warning. The predator may not be aware that there are any chimps around. A silent grin will not reveal where the chimp is hiding and will not let the predator know that there are other chimps nearby.

2. **B. A clenched fist.** Chimpanzees communicate with each other by sounds, gestures, and facial expressions. When a chimpanzee is frightened, it will grin. This is called a "fear grin." The chimp will bare its teeth and show its pink gums as a signal that it is ready to fight. The grin is used to scare off a rival or predator, but if that doesn't work, they may also shriek and scream. There are certain rules within the group of chimpanzees that all understand. If one chimp stares at another, slaps the ground, or shows its teeth, it is interpreted as a threatening gesture.

3. **C. If they have on their "play faces."** When two chimps play together, they may appear to be fighting or wrestling, but if they have on their "play faces," they are not angry. The play face is a smile, but the gums and teeth are covered by the lower lip.

4. **C. Takes medicine.** Over the years, researchers and natives have noted that chimps are aware of the different kinds of leaves found in the jungle and their medicinal properties. When some leaves are swallowed, they reduce parasites, while others kill bacteria, fungus, and viruses. When a chimp suffers from a certain illness, it is able to choose the kind of leaf that will cure it. Some chimps have even been observed crushing leaves and applying them on infected areas on their bodies.

5. **C. Grin.** Grinning is a behavior that warns of danger or is used to intimidate. Wild chimpanzees often bow and shake hands as a way of saying "hello." When chimpanzees meet after they have not seen each other for a long time, they may hug or kiss each other.

6. **D. Hunt.** Chimpanzees are basically vegetarians, but they sometimes hunt animals for food. In West Africa, groups of six adult chimpanzees will hunt for Colobus monkeys about once a week. The hunt is well-planned, with each member knowing its duty. One chimp will frighten the monkeys, and they will run away. There are older chimpanzees on either side of the retreating monkeys, so they can only run into the trap. The oldest chimp will be ahead of the group to catch the monkeys coming towards it. At the last moment, the oldest chimpanzee will turn, and the monkeys will be so frightened that they will stop for a moment, so the chimpanzees are able to catch them very easily. Monkeys aren't the only prey of chimpanzees—they also feed upon small birds, rabbits, young baboons, and basically any type of small animal that is available.

7. **B. Use tools.** Except for humans, no other animal uses as many different objects as tools as chimps do. Chimps not only use tools, they make them. Chimps often feed on termites by using a long twig, vine, or piece of grass. The chimp will get a twig, break it so that it is the right size, strip away the leaves on its end, put the twig into the termite nest, and wiggle it around. When it becomes covered with the insects, the chimp will pull it out and eat them off the twig. Chimps also use sticks to make the entrance to the termite nest larger, so the termites can be reached more easily. In West Africa, there are chimps that crack nuts and seeds by using stones as hammers. Some even chew leaves to make them more absorbent,

Mammals: Chimpanzees Answers (cont.)

so that they can dip water from holes in trees. Other chimps use leaves to clean themselves. West African chimps use stones to crack hard seeds. Chimpanzees may also use stones and sticks as missiles or clubs.

8. **A. Duck, Duck, Mongoose.**

9. **A. A minute.** Chimpanzees live in a tree house or nest that they make every night when they need to sleep. Each chimp, with the exception of infants that nest with their mothers, constructs a nest. It takes years of observation and practice for a chimp to learn how to make a nest. The chimp will first choose a tree with a strong bough that is about 30–40 feet off the ground for a foundation. It then stands on the bough and pulls three thick branches towards itself. While holding these branches with its feet, the chimp weaves them into a disc around the base, which will eventually be about 32 inches in diameter. It will then work smaller branches into a wreath and line it with leaves and twigs. Chimpanzees generally use their nests for only one night.

10. **B. Is treated well.** In some primate groups and among other kinds of mammals as well, an older dominant male who loses his dominance may be banished from the group. This is not true with chimpanzees. They are allowed to stay with their troop and are treated with respect. This may not just be kindness on the part of the other chimpanzees. These older males are respected because they know and remember where food is located and have other knowledge that can benefit the troop.

11. **A. Stop smoking.** Charlie, a male chimp, picked up cigarettes thrown to him by visitors and smoked. Zoo workers think he learned how to smoke by watching spectators. When zoo workers come near him, Charlie hides the cigarette.

Name: _____ Date: _____

Mammals: Gorillas

Gorillas are huge apes that live in Africa. While gorillas are often portrayed as aggressive, angry creatures, they are really shy and peaceful vegetarians. There are three kinds of gorillas: the western lowland gorilla, the eastern lowland gorilla, and the mountain gorilla. The loss of their habitat makes these majestic primates in great danger of becoming extinct.

Directions: Circle the letter of the correct answer(s).

1. Gorillas get most of the water they need from:
    A.   Streams and lakes.   B.   Rain.   C.   Plants.   D.   Wells.

2. Young gorillas like to play. Which of the following is *not* a game they play?
    A.   Follow the leader   B.   King of the mountain
    C.   Tag   D.   Who's got the banana?

3. Gorillas are apes, not monkeys. The way to distinguish between an ape and a monkey is that apes:
    A.   Are hairier.   B.   Do not have tails.
    C.   Do not live in trees.   D.   Are vegetarians.

4. The adult male gorilla is called:
    A.   A boar.   B.   A bull.   C.   A silverback.   D.   Man ape.

5. Humans' closest relative among the animals is the:
    A.   Chimpanzee.   B.   Gorilla.   C.   Monkey.   D.   Porpoise.

6. If a young adult male gorilla challenges the dominant male in the group and is successful, one of the first things he may do when he becomes the dominant male is to:
    A.   Get rid of all of the females.   B.   Establish a new territory.
    C.   Kill all of the children.   D.   Beat his chest and sing a song.

7. Which best describes a gorilla?
    A.   Ferocious   B.   Gentle   C.   Aggressive   D.   A loner

8. Humans can be positively identified by their unique fingerprints. Gorillas have unique:
    A.   Feet.   B.   Nose prints.   C.   Eyes.   D.   Earprints.

9. The Frankfurt, Germany, zoo put a television set in a gorilla's cage. Which of the following was *not* among the gorilla's favorite shows?
    A.   Love scenes   B.   Animal documentaries   C.   Racing   D.   Weight-lifting

10. Gorillas are vegetarians. It is estimated that an adult gorilla will need approximately how many pounds of food per day?
    A.   5 pounds   B.   25 pounds   C.   50 pounds   D.   100 pounds

Mammals: Gorillas Answers

1. **C. Plants.** Mountain gorillas are mainly vegetarian. They eat leaves, shoots, fruit, bulbs, bark, and nettles. These plants provide most of the moisture that a gorilla needs to survive.

2. **D. Who's got the banana?** Young gorillas like to run, tumble, and climb. They play follow the leader, king of the mountain, and tag as their mothers watch.

3. **B. Do not have tails.** Chimpanzees, gorillas, bonobos, and orangutans are called the great apes because they are large and look more like humans. They are more intelligent than monkeys and gibbons. Gibbons are called lesser apes. Apes are found in the tropical forests of Southeast Asia and western and central Africa. Apes are different from monkeys because they do not have a tail, they have a more complex brain, and they have an appendix.

4. **C. A silverback.** The biggest and strongest mature male gorilla is called a silverback because the hair on a male's back turns from black to silvery gray when he is between 11 and 13 years old. A silverback's group usually includes a subadult male or two and a few females and their young.

5. **A. Chimpanzee.** It is estimated that 98.4% of the genes in humans are the same as that of chimpanzees. Orangutans, another ape closely related to humans, share about 97% of their genetic makeup with humans. Because humans are not designed to live in trees, they stand and walk upright, unlike other primates. Chimpanzees suffer from many of the same diseases that humans suffer from. Chimps get ulcers and even arthritis. From time to time, a group of chimpanzees may even suffer from polio. When a chimpanzee dies, the family members will grieve. They may stay away from other chimps and sit, rocking back and forth, pulling out their hair. If a mother with a young chimp under five dies, it is likely that the young chimp will not survive.

6. **C. Kill all of the children.** Gorillas live in family groups that number from six to 30. These groups are led by one or two silverbacked males that are related to each other. They are usually a father and one or more of his sons. Adult females join the group, and the young are offspring of silverbacks. Males become mature at about nine years old, but they do not reproduce until they become about 12–15 years of age. Male gorillas leave their birth group and try to get females in order to form their own family group. The young male may invade another group and try to kidnap females. Sometimes a male will stay in his birth group and become its second silverback and eventually take over and become the dominant male when his father ages or dies. Or, he may challenge a silverback of another group. When a new silverback takes over a troop, he will sometimes kill all of the infants in the group so that the family will belong to him, and he will not have to care for another gorilla's children.

7. **B. Gentle.** Because of movies and books, the image most people have of a gorilla is that he is a ferocious, aggressive, mean creature that reveals its threat by pounding its chest, roaring, charging, and baring its teeth. Research has shown, however, that gorillas are peaceful, gentle, and social creatures that mainly eat vegetation. The ferocious displays are generally from a male gorilla who is trying to protect his family group.

8. **B. Nose prints.**

9. **B. Animal documentaries.** The gorillas enjoyed love scenes the most, weight-lifting next, and then racing.

10. **C. 50 pounds.**

Name: _____ Date: _____

Animals' Homes

Directions: Match the animal to its home. Some of these animals are not mammals.

Animals	**Homes**	**Use These Words**
1. A beaver lives in a	_____	mound
2. A baby kangaroo lives in a	_____	drey
3. An otter lives in a	_____	nest
4. A bat lives in a	_____	web
5. A rabbit lives in a	_____	snail shell
6. An ant lives in an ant	_____	pouch
7. A squirrel lives in a	_____	hill
8. A fox lives in a	_____	roost
9. A termite lives in a termite	_____	lodge
10. A spider lives in a	_____	sett
11. A bee lives in a	_____	warren
12. A mole lives in a	_____	hole
13. A hare lives in a	_____	den
14. A badger lives in a	_____	hive
15. A crocodile lives in a	_____	holt
16. A hermit crab lives in a	_____	form

Name: _____ Date: _____

Find the Mammals

Directions: Several mammals are hidden in these unusual sentences shown below. Find them by looking within words or between two or more words. Circle the names of the mammals. The first is given as a sample. There are at least 52 mammals hidden in the sentences. Some mammals will appear more than once.

1. Such are the facts of the case.
2. Supersize brakes stop big trucks.
3. Susan is such a chatterbox.
4. "You should tap irregular pickets," the boss explained.
5. There are approximately ten million bad germs in every sneeze.
6. He cannot be arrested in the chapel.
7. She visited the pyramids, which are enormous edifices.
8. The school decided to establish rewards for good attendance.
9. Wake up and attack the day.
10. A person should be happy with one's lot in life.
11. To be a rich man and have millions is a fantasy for many.
12. Jeb is on the job at 8:00 every day.
13. The park ranger would release a little chipmunk each day.
14. Cory X. Welk, from nearby Akron, was perfect.
15. James Stiger made an enormous effort to win.
16. People who win the lottery tend to brag.
17. Tom would always lose all patience.
18. No one wants to be average.
19. He was not terribly impressed with the cheap eraser.
20. Heraklion is the capital of the island and the largest city on Crete.
21. The newspaper reporter made errors in his story.
22. The acrobat stopped, tottered, and then fell.
23. Cliff Oxman wore a beard.
24. "He is such a cruel kid," the teacher said.
25. Missing his favorite dessert was a harsh reward for bad behavior.
26. Whenever possible, he would grab bits of chocolate.
27. Don't debate each other.
28. "Both are graduates from separate colleges," the proud mother said.
29. He sheepishly asked for a vacation.
30. He was not terribly impressed with the game.
31. He was pleased with the girl who greeted him warmly.
32. You could tell he was obnoxious by the way he filled out the application.
33. The coward became rattled when he ate horseradish.
34. Only evil people murder others.
35. Nice people do good.

Name: _____ Date: _____

Mammals: Orangutans

Orangutans are large apes that live in southeast Asia on the islands of Sumatra and Borneo. An orangutan has a large body, thick neck, very long, strong arms, short legs, and is about two-thirds the size of the gorilla. Orangutans spend most of their time in trees. They swing from branch to branch and leap between trees. When they do go down on the ground, they usually walk on all fours, but not easily, because their short legs are weak, and they don't have a heel bone. Orangutans are *omnivores*, which means they eat both plants and animals; however, they mostly eat plants. Their diet consists of fruit, leaves, seeds, flowers, plants, insects, and small mammals.

Directions: Circle the letter of the correct answer(s).

1. The orangutan is raised:
   A. In a single-parent family.
   C. By a group of aunts.
   B. In a male-dominated family.
   D. By its uncles.

2. The name "orangutan" in Mayla, the native language, means:
   A. Yetti.   B. Person of the forest.   C. Red ape.   D. Orange and tan ape.

3. The reason orangutans live alone is that:
   A. They are easy to anger.
   C. There are so few left.
   B. They smell so bad.
   D. So they won't starve.

4. Orangutans sleep in:
   A. Nests.   B. Caves.   C. Holes.   D. Bamboo huts.

5. Orangutans sometimes use items they find to make tools. Two things they may make are:
   A. Cups and umbrellas.
   C. Hammers and saws.
   B. Walking sticks and crutches.
   D. Maps and signs.

6. In order to keep other orangutans out of his territory, the male will let out a loud call that ends with:
   A. Screams.   B. Burps and sighs.   C. A song.   D. A whistle.

7. By the time orangutans become adults, one in three will have:
   A. A mate.   B. Its own territory.   C. A broken bone.   D. A family.

8. If a baby following its mother reaches a gap between trees that is too wide for it to cross, the mother will:
   A. Leave the baby behind.
   C. Make herself into a bridge.
   B. Scold the youngster until it jumps.
   D. Find another path without a gap.

9. When a number of orangutans come together to feed, the adults ignore one another while the youngsters:
   A. Cling to their mother.   B. Fight.   C. Sit by themselves.   D. Play.

Mammals: Orangutans Answers

1. **A. In a single-parent family.** Orangutans are not as sociable as other apes. They do not live in large social groups. Adult males are solitary creatures who stake out areas of forest, which they defend as their own, and fight other males who intrude. The males generally remain by themselves until they find a female who is willing to mate. After mating, the male will stay with the female for several days and then go back to his solitary life. The mother and offspring live together for about seven years, making it the longest childhood dependence on the mother of any animal in the world. It is important that the young ape stays with its mother a long time because there is so much for a young orangutan to learn in order to survive. Baby orangutans nurse until they are about six years old. While young males may stay close by their mothers for a few years after they are no longer nursing, females stay until they are into their teens. This gives them an opportunity to observe and learn mothering skills as they watch their younger brothers and sisters being raised by the mother.

2. **B. Person of the forest.** Male orangutans are able to make long, loud calls that carry throughout the forest. These calls serve three functions: they help the male claim his territory, keep out intruding males, and call to females. Males have a large throat sac that enables them to make these loud calls.

3. **D. So they won't starve.** Living alone is most likely due to their food requirements. Orangutans need a large area in order to get enough food. Too many orangutans in one area might lead to starvation. Orangutans have tremendous appetites. If they would travel in a group, they would quickly use up all of the food in a large area.

4. **A. Nests.** Every evening, orangutans will construct a "nest" in the branches of a tree. These nests are made out of leaves and branches and are shared by a mother and her nursing offspring. The orangutan will find a tree with branches that generally have three forks and are high off the ground. It will weave branches between them that will provide it support. Sometimes, the orangutan will make a roof out of a leaf to protect itself from the rain. Actually, most orangutans build two nests in trees each day. One is used for an afternoon nap, and the other is used when they sleep at night.

5. **A. Cups and umbrellas.** Orangutans are very intelligent. They have been known to use leaves as umbrellas to stay dry when it rains and leaves as cups to help them drink water.

6. **B. Burps and sighs.** Adult males need large territories in order to provide an adequate food supply. To warn others away from its territory, the orangutan will emit a series of short roars that ends with a series of burps and sighs. Sometimes the orangutan's roar is similar to that of a lion.

7. **C. A broken bone.** Orangutans spend most of their time in trees, and falling is a constant concern.

8. **C. Make herself into a bridge.** Orangutans have long, powerful arms and hook-shaped hands and feet, enabling them to climb and swing from tree to tree easily. They reach from one tree to the next and swing their bodies across the gap. The mother can make herself into a living bridge for the baby to cross.

9. **D. Play.** Even after an orangutan leaves its mother, it may socialize a bit with other orangutans it meets in the forest and may play or feed with them. As the orangutan becomes older, however, it will strike out on its own and become a solitary creature as its ancestors were.

Name: _____ Date: _____

Baby Mammals

Some mammals have special names given to their babies. Some baby names are used for more than one animal.

Directions: Write the name of the baby mammal for each species below.

Animals	Baby Names	Use These Words
1. A baby cow is called a(n)	_____	cub
2. A baby bear is called a(n)	_____	kitten
3. A baby deer is called a(n)	_____	kid
4. A baby beaver is called a(n)	_____	foal
5. A baby cat is called a(n)	_____	calf
6. A baby elephant seal is called a(n)	_____	joey
7. A baby goat is called a(n)	_____	fawn
8. A baby seal is called a(n)	_____	infant
9. A baby rabbit is called a(n)	_____	puggle
10. A baby sheep is called a(n)	_____	pinkie
11. A baby kangaroo is called a(n)	_____	kit
12. A baby pig is called a(n)	_____	lamb
13. A baby rat is called a(n)	_____	piglet
14. A baby whale is called a(n)	_____	leveret
15. A baby horse is called a(n)	_____	weaner
16. A baby elephant is called a(n)	_____	bunny
17. A baby fox is called a(n)	_____	pup
18. A baby zebra is called a(n)	_____	
19. A baby hare is called a(n)	_____	
20. A baby hedgehog is called a(n)	_____	
21. A baby monkey is called a(n)	_____	
22. A baby mouse is called a(n)	_____	
23. A baby echidna is called a(n)	_____	

Name: _____ Date: _____

Mammals: Lemurs

Lemurs are small primates found only on Madagascar and the Co-moro Islands. Lemurs have long hind limbs, large eyes, bodies similar to monkeys, a long bushy tail, and fur that can be brown, black, gray, or reddish. Lemurs are not as smart as monkeys, but their sense of smell is more acute. Lemurs are gregarious animals, and many species live in groups of ten or more. They sleep during the day and are active at night. Lemurs spend most of their time in the trees. They eat fruits, leaves, insects, eggs, and small birds.

Directions: Circle the letter of the correct answer(s).

1. The ring-tailed lemur, a primate found only on the island of Madagascar:
   A. Sings like a bird.
   C. Meows like a cat.
   B. Barks like a dog.
   D. Clucks like a chicken.

2. The aye-aye is a strange-looking lemur with large ears and brown fur. When local people see one of these creatures, they:
   A. Kill it.
   C. Follow it.
   B. Bow to it.
   D. Sing to it.

3. Among the ring-tailed lemurs, the males perform what job for the females?
   A. They are servants.
   C. They are teachers.
   B. They are hairdressers.
   D. They are entertainers.

4. The smallest primate is called a:
   A. Tom Thumb lemur.
   C. Lilliputian lemur.
   B. Munchkin lemur.
   D. Mouse lemur.

5. Much of the communication practiced by lemurs is done by:
   A. Sight.
   C. Touch.
   B. Sound.
   D. Smell.

6. When one troop of lemurs invades another troop's territory, a fight may erupt. Who leads the fight?
   A. Males
   C. Either males or females
   B. Females
   D. Children

7. When two lemurs meet and want to fight, they have a:
   A. Fist fight.
   C. Vocal fight.
   B. Stink fight.
   D. Pantomime fight.

8. The largest lemur is the indri. The word *indri* means:
   A. There it is.
   C. Large primate that lives in the trees.
   B. What is that?
   D. Big mouse.

Name: _____ Date: _____

Mammals: Lemurs (cont.)

9. In a troop of ring-tailed lemurs, the rulers are:
    A. Females.   B. Males.
    C. Both males and females.   D. Children.

10. The indri lemur spends most of its life in the trees. It only comes down to the ground to:
    A. Go to the bathroom.   B. Fight.
    C. Eat dirt or bark.   D. Drink.

11. Black lemurs protect themselves from parasites by:
    A. Grooming.   B. Eating them.
    C. Diet.   D. Rubbing on an insect repellent.

12. The social ranking of lemurs can be determined by observing their:
    A. Baby lemurs.   B. Heads and tails.
    C. Food.   D. Mate's hand.

13. The word *lemur* means:
    A. Ghost or spirit.   B. Monkey boy.
    C. Child of the forest.   D. Smelly monkey.

Mammals: Lemurs Answers

1. **C. Meows like a cat.**
2. **A. Kill it.** The natives believe that this lemur has magical powers and that if they see an aye-aye and do not kill it, someone in their village will die. For this reason, there are few aye-aye left.
3. **B. They are hairdressers.** Females are the ones who get the grooming. The males are the ones who always offer to groom them.
4. **D. Mouse lemur.** It weighs only 1 1/2 to 3 ounces.
5. **D. Smell.** While most primates get most of their information visually, lemurs receive a lot of their information through scent. The lemur has scent glands in different places on its body, and there is a special organ located on the roof of its mouth that is used to detect chemicals released by the scent glands. Between the elbow and the wrist is a special gland that is similar to a human's armpit. And like a human's armpit, there is a scent that the lemur uses to "mark" its territory. The lemur will move its arm against a tree branch in order to let other lemurs know that it is around. What do the scents communicate to other lemurs? They express information about breeding, families, and territory boundaries.
6. **B. Females.** Females do not subordinate themselves to the males, as other primates do. Females get the best sleeping spots and often lead fights by attacking invading troops. They fight with their teeth and their hands. On the other hand, males try to intimidate their rivals with their strong odor. If there is a disagreement between a male and a female lemur, the female always wins.
7. **B. Stink fight.** The lemur has a long, striped tail that it holds up straight when it wants to signal its readiness to fight. Its armpits produce smelly secretions that are used to rub on its tail. When the fight begins, the lemurs advance toward each other waving their tails in the air in an attempt to make the scent so disgusting that the other male will retreat. This is known as a stink fight.
8. **A. There it is.** The largest lemur still in existence is the indri, which literally means "there it is" in the local language. The indri, which looks like a giant teddy bear, is active during the day as it forages for fruit and leaves. It spends most of its life in the trees and only comes down to the ground occasionally.
9. **A. Females.**
10. **C. Eat dirt or bark.** Researchers believe that eating dirt or bark may be an aid to digestion.
11. **D. Rubbing on an insect repellent.** When millipedes are wounded or threatened, they release toxic chemicals that include hydrogen cyanide, chlorine, and iodine. Black lemurs have learned that if they bite into millipedes and then rub the wounded body on their fur, they will not be bothered by parasites.
12. **B. Heads and tails.** Some female lemurs rank higher than other females. The same is true among the males in a troop. They fight each other in order to determine rank. Lower-ranked lemurs keep their tails and heads down as they move through the troop, while higher-ranking males will strut around with their heads and tails held high.
13. **A. Ghost or spirit.** The word "lemur" comes from the Latin word, *lemurs*, which means "spirits of the dead." The Latin name was given to these creatures because of the way they move quietly through the trees at night.

Name: _____ Date: _____

Mammals: Lions

The lion is a 500-pound cat with a long, strong body, short legs, and huge head. The male is about seven feet long, not including its tail. It is about four feet tall at the shoulders. The female, or lioness, stands a foot shorter and weighs over 100 pounds less. The one characteristic that identifies the male, other than its size, is its mane. The size, shape, and color of the mane vary from lion to lion, but it frames the lion's face and gives the animal a regal appearance.

Although the lion is smaller than a tiger, it is still referred to as the "king of beasts." Lions are found mainly in parts of Africa, although a few hundred lions live under protection in the Gir Forest National Park in Gujarat State, India. Lions prefer to live on grassy plains and open savannas.

Directions: Circle the letter of the correct answer(s).

1. Lions that live in Kenya rest in:
   A. Trees.   B. Caves.   C. Lakes.   D. Hammocks.

2. Who hunts the animals upon which the lions feed?
   A. Male lion   B. Female lion   C. Teams of males   D. Teams of females

3. When lions and tigers mate, what do you call their cubs?
   A. Liger   B. Tigons   C. Tiglons   D. Sigfrieds

4. A group of lions living together is called:
   A. A family.   B. A herd.   C. A pride.   D. Lots 'o lions.

5. When males are forced to leave the pride into which they were born, they form small bachelor groups and roam. These groups are called:
   A. An alliance.   B. A confederacy.   C. A coalition.   D. A league.

6. When a female lion goes hunting, her cubs often:
   A. Are left with a babysitter.   B. Are watched by the males.
   C. Go on the hunt.   D. Are placed in a tree.

7. The greatest threats to lion cubs are:
   A. Hyenas.   B. Leopards.   C. Lions.   D. Humans.

8. Females in the pride will often give birth:
   A. To six cubs at a time.   B. Every six months.
   C. In the spring.   D. At the same time.

9. When lions walk, their heels:
   A. Touch the ground first.   B. Touch the ground last.
   C. Don't touch the ground.   D. Touch ground at the same time as their toes.

10. The term "lion's share" originally meant:
    A. All of something.   B. The largest portion of something.
    C. The smallest portion of something.   D. None.

Mammals: Lions Answers

1. **A. Trees.** The lions that live in the Masai Mara, an area of Kenya, are very unusual. They climb trees and stretch out on the branches.

2. **D. Teams of females.** The male lion is bigger and stronger than the female. His main duty is to defend the pride's territory. His roar, which can carry for five miles, warns intruders. While males hunt occasionally, the females do most of the hunting. Their hunt is carefully planned with each member understanding the part it must play in order to be successful. The team of females first finds a group of zebras, antelope, or other animals. They often single out a young, old, or weakened animal that will be easier to catch. While one female quietly goes to the far side of the herd, the others lie down on their bellies with their eyes focused on the prey. Then they slowly inch towards the victim. If the victim shows any sign that it is being stalked, the lions will freeze until the victim relaxes. Surprising the prey is important since the animals they stalk cannot only run faster, they can run longer than the lion. When they are as close as they can be without being detected, the female lions launch their attack. The victim naturally tries to run away but instead runs directly into the reach of the lone female. She grabs the animal by the neck, and the others jump on its back, wrestling it to the ground. For all of their planning, lionesses aren't successful hunters. They miss more kills than they make. After the kill, the males usually eat first, lionesses eat next, and the cubs eat what's left.

3. **A., B., C.** They are called ligers when the father is a lion and tigons or tiglons when the father is a tiger.

4. **C. A pride.** From three to 30 lions live in a **pride**. All of the females in a pride are related. When the male cubs grow up, they will leave their pride and travel with other young males.

5. **C. A coalition.** The young males join a **coalition** that will eventually take over a pride of females. After a period of two to four years, another male coalition will kick these males out of the pride and take over.

6. **A. Are left with a babysitter.** The babysitter is paid with part of the hunt.

7. **C. Lions.** Lion cubs are sometimes killed by hyenas and leopards. The greatest danger to cubs, however, is from adult male lions. This often occurs when a new male coalition takes over a pride. The new coalition realizes that since they will only be with the pride from two to four years before they are replaced by a new coalition, they must begin to breed, so that all future cubs will have their genes. However, this poses a problem. Females will not mate until their cubs are at least 18 months old. So, males kill all the young cubs so that the females will be ready to mate sooner. In some cases, older cubs might escape before they are killed. If they do escape, they are on their own and will not have a pride for protection and food. Sometimes mothers will leave with the young cubs and remain away from the pride until the cubs are old enough to join a pride or a coalition. While female lions would never kill the young cubs of other females in their own prides, they do kill the cubs of females in other prides.

8. **D. At the same time.** This ability is unique to lions. The young cubs are reared by the entire pride. They are nursed by any female who is close by. Lions are more sociable than most believe. They are very affectionate and playful with others in their pride.

9. **C. Don't touch the ground.**

10. **A. All of something.**

Name: _____ Date: _____

Mammals: Other Big Cats

Lions, tigers, leopards, snow leopards, cheetahs, and jaguars are all considered "big cats." There are five subspecies of tiger. They are the Bengal, South China, Indo-Chinese, Sumatran, and Siberian. Three subspecies of tiger are extinct: the Caspian, Bali, and Javan. Leopards are found in Africa and Asia. Cheetahs originally lived in an area from North Africa to India, but they are now commonly found only south of the Sahara Desert. Jaguars are often confused with leopards because they look similar, but jaguars live in South America. The lion, another of the big cats, is covered in another section of this book.

Directions: Circle the letter of the correct answer(s).

1. Wild tigers eat:
   A. Every day.
   C. 40 pounds of meat at a time.
   B. Mainly vegetables.
   D. Other tigers.

2. Tigers have:
   A. Stripes.
   C. Stripes and striped skin.
   B. Striped skin.
   D. Stripes and spots.

3. Tigers are mostly located in:
   A. Asia.
   C. Circuses.
   B. Europe.
   D. Zoos.

4. A cheetah is capable of running:
   A. 20 miles per hour.
   C. 60 miles per hour.
   B. 40 miles per hour.
   D. 80 miles per hour.

5. The main reason the cheetah is able to run so fast is because of its:
   A. Slim body.
   C. Spine.
   B. Long tail.
   D. Claws.

6. A cheetah mother teaches her cubs to hunt by using:
   A. A live gazelle calf.
   C. Other cubs.
   B. Her tail.
   D. A dead gazelle.

7. Cheetah cubs do not need to hide from their predators because:
   A. Their mother protects them.
   C. They look like honey badgers.
   B. Their father protects them.
   D. They have a foul smell.

Name: _____ Date: _____

Mammals: Other Big Cats (cont.)

8. What is the only member of the cat family that does not have retractable claws?
    A. Lion   B. Leopard
    C. Cheetah   D. Lynx

9. What is a group of leopards called?
    A. Leap   B. Pride
    C. Host   D. Pod

10. The snow leopard protects itself from extreme cold when it sleeps by:
    A. Snuggling with its mate.   B. Wrapping its tail around its nose.
    C. Building a cave in the snow.   D. Making a den out of branches.

11. After a kill, the cheetah will:
    A. Feed immediately.   B. Bury the kill.
    C. Let the cubs eat first.   D. Rest.

12. When a cheetah chases an animal, if the chase is not short, the cheetah may suffer:
    A. Death.   B. Stomach cramps.
    C. Brain damage.   D. Temporary blindness.

13. A leopard stores its kill:
    A. In a hole in the ground.   B. Under bushes.
    C. In a tree.   D. Underwater.

Mammals: Other Big Cats Answers

1. **C. 40 pounds of meat at a time.** Some wild tigers can eat up to 40 pounds of meat at a time and not eat again for several days. Tigers have been known to eat up to 60 pounds of meat in one night, but more often they consume about 12 pounds during a meal. It may take days for a tiger to finish eating its kill. The cat eats until it's full and then covers the carcass with leaves and dirt. When it's hungry again, the tiger comes back to feed some more until the meat is gone.
2. **C. Stripes and striped skin.** No two tigers have exactly the same pattern of stripes.
3. **A. Asia.** Tigers are mostly located in Asia. The reason the tigers are becoming endangered is because of the loss of their habitat due to the spread of man and because of poaching. Tiger skins and body parts are considered valuable and used as medicines in some parts of the world. They are illegal to own in most civilized nations. It is estimated that soon there will be more tigers in zoos and circuses than in the wild.
4. **C. 60 miles per hour.** From a standing start, a cheetahs can accelerate to 45 miles per hour in three seconds. It can run over 60 miles per hour but cannot maintain this speed very long. If it does not catch its prey quickly, it may give up the chase and rest.
5. **C. Spine.** Its incredibly flexible spine acts like kind of a spring. The spine curls and uncurls, pushing the cheetah forward. Its tail acts as a counterbalance for the body as it runs.
6. **A. A live gazelle calf.** A cheetah mother will catch a live gazelle calf so her cubs can practice hunting. She releases the calf in front of the cubs, and when it makes a dart for freedom, the cubs try to chase it and bring it down. If the calf escapes, the mother will catch it and begin the lesson again. During these practice sessions, the cubs learn how to stalk and bring down prey with their forepaws and how to kill by biting the throat.
7. **C. They look like honey badgers.** While adult big cats are feared, their cubs are small, defenseless, and vulnerable. They can be caught and eaten by predators. Some species of cat cubs have coats that act as a camouflage, but cheetah cubs are not so lucky. For the first few first weeks of life, a cheetah cub develops a thick coat called a mantle. While the dark color offers some protection by enabling the cub to blend into the shadows, the real value of the mantle is that it resembles the fur of a honey badger, a vicious small predator that is left alone by most other predators. The mantle begins to disappear when the cub is about three months old, but there are some last traces of it at over two years of age.
8. **C. Cheetah.** Unlike other big cats, the cheetah's claws are permanently exposed.
9. **A. Leap.** This is sometimes spelled *leep*.
10. **B. Wrapping its tail around its nose.** Its tail is three feet long.
11. **D. Rest.** The cheetah does not feed immediately after a kill. It needs about a half-hour to rest and pant in order to cool down before it can eat. Then it gulps its food quickly so that a leopard, lion, or hyena cannot eat it before the cheetah does.
12. **C. Brain damage.** The chase by a cheetah must be short. An average chase lasts less than 20 seconds. The cheetah's powerful muscles, combined with the hot African temperature, generate an enormous amount of heat. During a 200-yard chase, the body temperature of a cheetah can rise to well over 100°F. If the chase continues for a minute or longer, the heat can rise and cause brain damage.
13. **C. In a tree.** After a kill, a leopard will eat its fill and then pull the remaining carcass into a tree so it will be safe from hyenas and jackals.

59

Name: _____ Date: _____

Mythbuster: Rodents

Directions: Shown on the following page are a number of questions and statements concerning rodents. Fill in the spaces below with the correct word that goes with the statement. Then take the letters in the circle and put them in the spaces below the puzzle. The words that are spelled from these letters explain a myth about rats: They don't _____ _____ _____.

1.
2.
3.
4.
5.
6. 
7.
8.
9. 
10.
11.
12.
13.
14.
15.
16.
17.
18.

Answer: __ __ __ __   __ __ __ __ __ __   __ __ __ __ __.

Name: _____ Date: _____

Mythbuster: Rodents (cont.)

1. This rodent is also called the groundhog or the whistle-pig. It is a member of the squirrel family and is found across Canada and in the northeastern and midwestern United States.

2. This animal lives in and near water. It has a flat tail and attractive shiny fur. It is known for building dams.

3. This is an order of animals that includes beavers, rats, and mice.

4. This rodent is large with dense, glossy fur that is dark brown above and lighter on its sides. This animal is a lot like the beaver but is a few inches smaller. It has webbed hind feet and uses its rudder-like tail for steering. This rodent's house is similar to American beaver lodges, but much smaller. Part of its name comes from the musk glands located near the underside of its tail.

5. This is the unusual name for a baby mouse.

6. Many think this little, furry creature found in suburban yards is a rodent, but it isn't. It also doesn't leave colored eggs at Easter.

7. Homeowners set traps for this small rodent. It is also the name of something with which you operate your computer.

8. This mammal looks like a flying mouse.

9. This is another name for a woodchuck. On February 2nd, people think it can predict how long the winter will last.

10. A favorite food of squirrels, they often gather them in the fall and bury them to eat at a later time.

11. Often kept in cages as pets, these small rodents have short, rounded ears and no tail. Some are completely white, black, or tawny. They may also be streaked or blotched. They begin to breed at two months of age. They have been used as experimental laboratory animals. Their name consists of two words. The second name would lead you to believe that it was a farm animal.

12. This is the name for a group of beavers.

13. A large rodent that weighs about 22 pounds, it protects itself with over 30,000 quills that are from 1 to 2.5 inches in length. Its rump is covered with tiny, scalelike barbs.

14. These rodents are found in parks and live mainly in trees. They mainly eat nuts, seeds, and other vegetation.

Name: _____ Date: _____

Mythbuster: Rodents (cont.)

15. Rodents also belong to this group of animals that are covered with hair or fur and feed their young milk. Most give birth to live babies.

16. These are small, burrowing rodents that have soft, sandy-colored fur. They are sometimes called sand rats or desert rats because they are found in dry, sandy areas. Along with mice, hamsters, rats, and guinea pigs, these are often sold in pet stores and kept in cages. They can live up to eight years in captivity and often have litters of one to 14. They give birth to young as often as once a month for the first two years.

17. Part of the squirrel family—some varieties are called ground squirrels. They often have broad stripes down their backs. You may have heard of a group of these rodents that sings songs. Their leader is Alvin.

18. This is a small, burrowing mammal with a pointed snout; soft, thick fur; short legs; and long, powerful claws on the front pair of legs. Hated by homeowners, it digs burrows underground searching for earthworms and insect larvae. It can dig its tunnels very quickly.

Name: _____ Date: _____

Mammals: Bears

Bears are large mammals that can be found throughout the world. They have large bodies, short legs, a short tail, small, round ears, and they walk on their heels like humans. Bears are classified as carnivores, which means they eat the flesh of other animals, but each species of bear also eats plants to some degree. The polar bear is almost entirely a carnivore, while the panda is almost exclusively a herbivore (plant-eater).

Directions: Circle the letter of the correct answer(s).

1. The female brown bear gives birth while:
   A.   Sleeping.   B.   Running.   C.   Walking.   D.   Swimming.

2. Male bears are called:
   A.   Bucks.   B.   Stags.   C.   Papa Bears.   D.   Boars.

3. The polar bear is able to swim between ice floes that are how far apart?
   A.   10 miles   B.   20 miles   C.   40 miles   D.   60 miles

4. Polar bears are capable of traveling how far in search of food?
   A.   62 miles   B.   162 miles   C.   620 miles   D.   1,620 miles

5. A polar bear's skin is:
   A.   White.   B.   Black.   C.   Yellow.   D.   Pink.

6. A polar bear's fur is:
   A.   White.   B.   Transparent.   C.   Tan.   D.   Pink.

7. The largest carnivorous (meat-eating) mammal in the world is the:
   A.   Elephant.   B.   Giant panda bear.
   C.   Polar bear.   D.   Hippopotamus.

8. When a panda is born, it about the same size as a:
   A.   Flea.   B.   Mouse.
   C.   Dog.   D.   Pony.

9. The Chinese name for panda is *daxiongmao*, which means:
   A.   Black and white bear.   B.   Large bearcat.
   C.   Man of the forest.   D.   Child of God.

10. Pandas eat almost nothing but:
    A.   Eucalyptus.   B.   Small rodents.
    C.   Bamboo.   D.   Fish.

Mammals: Bears Answers

1. **A. Sleeping.** When the female brown bear begins her hibernation, she is pregnant. The large amount of fat she has stored is needed in order for the embryo of the baby or babies to develop normally. During the middle of her hibernation, the cub or cubs are born without hair and without the ability to see. They have only enough strength to begin nursing. By the time the mother awakes in the spring, the cub or cubs are strong enough to follow her as she leaves her den. About half of the brown bear cubs die before they are one year old. While mother brown bears are fiercely protective, cubs are in danger from mountain lions, wolves, and even their own fathers. Others starve to death or die of disease. A cub will stay with its mother for up to three years before it is able to leave and begin life on its own.
2. **D. Boars.**
3. **D. 60 miles.** Polar bears live along shores and on the ice in the Arctic. When the weather becomes colder and the ice forms over the ocean, male polar bears go onto the ice to hunt seals. When the weather becomes warm again and the ice melts, polar bears move back toward shore. The polar bear is a marine mammal that can swim between ice floes that are 60 miles apart without pausing for a rest. The bear's front paws are about 12 inches in diameter and are partially webbed between the toes, so it can swim at about six mph. The thick layers of blubber and fur not only insulate the bear and keep it warm, they also help make the bear buoyant.
4. **C. 620 miles.**
5. **B. Black.** While polar bears have fur that appears white, their skin is black. Their thick fur hides its color. The polar bear's fur, which appears to be white, turns yellowish during the summer.
6. **B. Transparent.** A polar bear's fur is not really white. Each hair shaft is transparent with a hollow core and has no color. It looks white because the hollow hair shaft scatters and reflects visible light, just as snow does.
7. **C. Polar bear.** Many disagree about which is the largest bear on Earth. Most believe it is the polar bear, but if that is true, then the Alaskan brown bear is a very close second. Brown bears, or grizzlies as they are sometimes called, eat mostly vegetation, but they also eat the meat of small mammals and fish when available. Polar bears, which can weigh as much as 1,500 pounds, primarily eat seals. The polar bear uses its excellent senses of smell and hearing to find seals that are several yards beneath the ice. It locates the seal's breathing hole and then waits for the seal to surface for air and captures it.
8. **B. Mouse.** The panda bear is one of the most attractive and recognizable animals in the world. The bear, which is black and white, makes its home in southwestern China. An adult male panda may be six feet in length and can weigh 275 pounds, but a newborn weighs only 4 ounces—about the same size as a mouse.
9. **B. Large bearcat.**
10. **C. Bamboo.** Pandas eat almost nothing but bamboo shoots and leaves. Pandas occasionally eat other vegetation, fish, or small animals, but bamboo accounts for 99 percent of their diets. Bamboo is not very nutritious, so pandas eat fast and spend about 12 hours a day eating. They usually eat about 15 percent of their weight each day, but when feeding on new bamboo shoots, they can eat up to 40 percent of their average body weight. How many pounds of food would you have to eat a day to eat 40 percent of your weight?

Name: _____ Date: _____

Mammals: Dogs

The domestic dog is closely related to wolves, jackals, and coyotes, and is able to breed with them and produce offspring. Dogs are usually considered the first domesticated animals. They have lived with humans as working partners and pets since the days of the cave-dwellers.

Directions: Circle the letter of the correct answer(s).

1. Henry III of France liked dogs so much he:
   A. Gave one a castle.   B. Appointed one as his chancellor.
   C. Adopted one as his son.   D. Wore a basket of them around his neck.

2. In the Solomon Islands, which of the following was once used as a form of currency?
   A. Dog teeth   B. Dog hides
   C. Puppy-dog tails   D. Dog paws

3. The breed of dog known as the Great Dane originated in:
   A. Denmark.   B. Germany.
   C. Great Britain.   D. Australia.

4. A substance that can be fatal to dogs is:
   A. Sugar.   B. Peppermint.
   C. Chocolate.   D. Caramel.

5. The Catahoula leopard dog is unusual because it:
   A. Has webbed feet.   B. Lays eggs.
   C. Doesn't chase its tail.   D. Barks with an accent.

6. During the sixteenth century, Norwegian farmers developed a breed of dog to hunt puffins. Which of the following characteristics does it *not* have?
   A. It can swivel its head and face to its back.   B. It can close its eardrums.
   C. It has six toes on each paw.   D. It can go weeks without eating.

7. In ancient times, the Chinese crested dog was used for:
   A. Medicine.   B. A heating pad.
   C. A religious charm.   D. Telling fortunes.

8. A Kerry blue terrier is always born:
   A. Blue.   B. White.   C. Black.   D. Yellow.

9. The chow is the only dog that has:
   A. Two left feet.   B. A black tongue.
   C. Striped fur.   D. Five toes.

10. In what country did the French poodle originate?
    A. France   B. Denmark   C. Germany   D. Transylvania

Mammals: Dogs Answers

1. **D. Wore a basket of them around his neck.** In the Middle Ages, King Henry III of France was so fond of his bichon frisés, that he would take several of them everywhere he went. He would carry them in a kind of basket around his neck. The king was not so fond of cats. If he happened to see a cat, the king would faint.

2. **A. Dog's teeth.**

3. **B. Germany.**

4. **C. Chocolate.** Chocolate contains theobromine, a chemical that can kill dogs if they eat enough. However, the amount of chocolate that it takes to kill a dog will vary by the size of the dog and the amount of theobromine in the chocolate.

5. **A. Has webbed feet.** Found in the Catahoula Lakes of Louisiana, the Catahoula leopard dog has webbed feet and very often has white eyes. When the Spanish conquerors came to the New World, they brought a breed of dog called the mastiff. Some of these dogs were abandoned and were adopted by the American Indians. The mastiffs mated with the Indians' dogs, and the Catahoula leopard dog was the offspring. Because the Catahoula has webbed feet, it is a good swimmer. Some people call them cow dogs because they help cowboys round up cattle.

6. **D. Go weeks without eating.** During the sixteenth century, Norwegian farmers developed a breed of dog to hunt puffins. Puffins are small seabirds that spend most of their time at sea in the North Atlantic. The Norwegian farmers named the new breed, "Lundehund." The name Lundehund is a combination of two Norwegian words "lunde," the word for puffin bird, and "hund," the word for dog. The Lundehund has the ability to close its eardrums in order to keep out the water and snow as it chases the puffins. It is able to turn its head completely around and face its back. It has six toes on each paw, which is helpful as it runs across the ice and up the cliffs to capture the puffin. The puffin bird became a protected species in the 1800s, and so the need for the dog was eliminated. Since there was no practical use for the Lundehund, they were no longer bred and may have become extinct had it not been for the work of concerned Norwegians.

7. **B. A heating pad.** The Chinese crested dogs are very rare. They do not have hair. They are small dogs with skin that may be pink, blue, lavender, or black. The dogs are lively and playful. In ancient times, these dogs were used as heating pads. A person with a sore muscle might put one of the dogs on that muscle in order to warm it up.

8. **C. Black.** The Kerry blue terrier is a medium-sized terrier. It is born black, but the coat changes color as it ages. It goes from black to dark blue and to different shades of blue-gray.

9. **B. A black tongue.** The tongues of all other dogs are pink.

10. **C. Germany.** Breed historians generally agree that the poodle had its origins in Germany, with some influence from Russia. It did, however, become standardized as a specific breed in France. That is why people refer to the poodle as the "French poodle." The name, "poodle" is taken from the German word *pudel,* which means "to splash in water." The French call the poodle the "Caniche," or duck dog. The poodle was originally used to retrieve waterfowl. Its unusual haircut is not just to look good. The legs are clipped so that there is less drag on them when the dog swims after a downed waterfowl. Hair is left long on the chest to protect the chest and heart from the cold weather. Hair is also left on the leg joints to protect them from the cold and from sharp reeds.

Name: _____ Date: _____

Dog Idioms

Directions: An **idiom** is a figure of speech or an expression that is sometimes used to express an idea. Listed below is a group of expressions that use the word *dog* or refer to a dog. Under each idiom, explain in your own words what the expression means.

1. Put on the dog. _____

_____

2. A barking dog never bites. _____

_____

3. You can't teach an old dog new tricks. _____

_____

4. Every dog has its day. _____

_____

5. Gone to the dogs _____

_____

6. Sick as a dog _____

_____

7. Underdog _____

_____

8. The tail wagging the dog _____

_____

9 In the doghouse _____

_____

10. If you lie down with dogs, you will get up with fleas. _____

_____

11. His bark is worse than his bite. _____

_____

12. A dog and pony show _____

_____

13. Let sleeping dogs lie. _____

_____

14. Treat somebody like a dog _____

_____

Name: _____ Date: _____

Mammals: Cats

Cats were domesticated in prehistoric times. Some experts believe that they have been domesticated for over 5,000 years. Humans brought cats into their homes not only for companionship, but also to kill snakes, mice, and rats. Ancient Egyptians considered cats sacred. Cats were also highly prized by the ancient Greeks and Romans for their ability to control rodents. However, during the Middle Ages in Europe, cats were the target of superstition. Hundreds of thousands of cats were tortured and killed because people thought they were witches or were associated with witchcraft. The elimination of so many cats resulted in an increase in the rodent population that, in turn, contributed to the spread of a form of the bubonic plague called the *black death,* a disease that is transmitted to people by the fleas on rats. In the fourteenth century, almost one-fourth of the entire population of Europe was killed by the plague.

Directions: Circle the letter of the correct answer(s).

1. A cat uses what part of its body in order "see" when it is totally dark?
   A. Fur   B. Tail   C. Whiskers   D. Tongue

2. Catgut is made from:
   A. Cat's intestines.   B. Sheep's intestines.   C. Nylon.   D. Plastic.

3. Cats were considered sacred animals in Ancient Egypt, and when they died, people mourned them by:
   A. Having them stuffed.   B. Eating them.
   C. Shaving off their own eyebrows.   D. Burning them at the temple.

4. There is a cat in Scotland called the Scottish fold cat. It has ears like:
   A. A jackrabbit's.   B. A hound dog's.   C. Flat tires.   D. Silver dollars.

5. Cats have been on the payroll of the British Post Office since the mid-1800s in order to:
   A. Keep down the rodent population.   B. Detect gas.
   C. Detect burglars.   D. Provide companionship.

6. The Sphynx, a breed of cat, is unique because it:
   A. Has three legs.   B. Has no hair.
   C. Has no whiskers.   D. Weighs only three ounces.

7. The manx is a domestic cat that:
   A. Has no tail.   B. Is tan with black spots.
   C. Is as large as a Great Dane. D. Has no teeth.

8. In 1950, a young cat did something no other cat had ever been known to do. The cat:
   A. Learned to speak 58 words.   B. Gave birth to 21 kittens.
   C. Climbed the Matterhorn.   D. Saved the president's life.

68

Mammals: Cats Answers

1. **C. Whiskers.** A cat's whiskers are long, tough hairs and are arranged in four rows on both sides of the cat's nose. Most cats have about twenty-four whiskers that are thicker than ordinary hairs, set deep, and have nerve endings that allow them to be aware of anything they touch. Whiskers also enable a cat to sense vibrations in air currents so they can sense objects without even touching them with their whiskers. If a cat's whiskers are damaged, the cat can become confused and uncomfortable.

2. **B. Sheep's intestines.** Catgut is a thin but tough cord that is made from the stretched intestines of some animals such as sheep and horses, but not cats. Catgut is used as the strings for musical instruments such as the harp and violin. Catgut is also used for stringing tennis rackets, and surgeons use it to close up some incisions.

3. **C. Shaving off their own eyebrows.** Animals were worshipped in Ancient Egypt because the people believed that animals were in close contact with the gods. It is likely that cats in Egypt were domesticated and brought into the homes originally to keep the homes free of rodents and snakes. Eventually, the cat was considered to be a god. Cats were not only protected by every Egyptian, they were also protected by the government. If someone killed a cat, even accidently, he or she was sentenced to death. When a cat died, its owners would mourn and shave their eyebrows as a sign of grief. Cats were often mummified. When put in tombs, the mummified cats were given mice, rats, and bowls of milk. Cats were so honored by the Egyptians that it once cost them a battle. The Egyptians were at war with the Persians. Knowing that the Egyptians worshipped cats, the Persian general ordered his men to collect as many cats as they could. The soldiers then released the cats on the battlefield. The Egyptians surrendered their city to the Persians rather than cause any harm to the cats.

4. **C. Flat tires.** The Scottish fold cat is a medium-sized cat with a well-rounded, padded look to its body. A fold cat has small, tightly folded ears that are rounded on the tip. The first Scottish fold cat was discovered in 1961 on a farm in Scotland.

5. **A. Keep down the rodent population.** In 1868, the Secretary of the British Post Office hired three female cats and paid them four pence a week each to keep down the rodent population. They were so successful that more were hired. In 1953, the Assistant Postmaster General spoke at the House of Commons and said that his female cats got very adequate maternity benefits and were paid wages equal to those of the tomcats.

6. **B. Has no hair.** The Sphynx is a breed of hairless cat. The first hairless cats were born naturally without hair. In other words, they were not bred to have this feature. In the 1960s, people began breeding Sphynx cats. In addition to its hairlessness, the Sphynx cat is known for its playful disposition.

7. **A. Has no tail.** The manx cat originated hundreds of years ago on the Isle of Man, off the coast of England. The gene that makes the Manx tailless is dominant. But this does not mean that all kittens born from a manx will not have a tail. In any given litter, some of the cats may be born without a tail, while others may have short or long tails.

8. **C. Climbed the Matterhorn.** The young cat climbed the Matterhorn by following some human climbers. The Matterhorn is one of the most popular mountains to climb in the Alps. It can be reached from Switzerland or Italy. It is over 14,000 feet high, and the death rate of those who attempt to climb it is one of the highest in the world. The climbers brought the cat back down with them.

Name: _____ Date: _____

Cat Idioms

Directions: An **idiom** is a figure of speech or an expression that is sometimes used to express an idea. Listed below is a group of expressions that use the word *cat*. Under each idiom, explain in your own words what the expression means.

1. Looked like the cat that ate the canary _____

    _____

2. The cat's pajamas _____

    _____

3. Looks like something the cat dragged in _____

    _____

4. Raining cats and dogs _____

    _____

5. There's more than one way to skin a cat. _____

    _____

6. When the cat's away, the mice will play. _____

    _____

7. Playing cat and mouse _____

    _____

8. Has the cat got your tongue? _____

    _____

9. Fight like cats and dogs _____

    _____

10. Let the cat out of the bag _____

    _____

11. Grinning like a Cheshire cat _____

    _____

12. Not enough room to swing a cat _____

    _____

13. A catnap _____

    _____

14. Curiosity killed the cat. _____

    _____

Name: _____ Date: _____

Mammals: Horses

The animal that eventually became the horse appeared first on the North American continent many years ago. It was about the size of a fox. This creature evolved into a larger animal, and its toes eventually became a hoof. It gradually evolved into the horse we know today. Horses lived on the North American continent as they were evolving. Although scientists do not know why, horses began leaving North America many years ago. They walked across the Bering Strait, through Asia, the Middle East, Europe, and Africa. Eventually, there were no more horses in North America.

About 4,000 to 5,000 years ago, the horse was domesticated by humans. Once tamed, horses served a variety of purposes. Horses carried hunters, travelers, and soldiers. Humans also discovered that if the horse was hitched to a plow, they were able to increase their agricultural abilities.

Horses were reintroduced into North and South America in 1519 when Cortés came from Spain. More Spanish and other Europeans arrived and brought horses with them. Horses had returned to their native land.

Directions: Circle the letter of the correct answer(s).

1. All racehorses in the United States celebrate their birthday on:
   A. The day they were born.   B. January 1st.
   C. The first day of the racing season.   D. July 4th.

2. Horses are the reason that:
   A. U.S. cars drive on the right.   B. Cars have horns.
   C. A polio vaccine was discovered.   D. Firehouses have circular staircases.

3. Which of the following is *not* a reason that humans first domesticated the wild horse?
   A. To use its meat for food   B. For its milk
   C. Transporting goods   D. Riding

4. How much horsepower does the average horse provide?
   A. 1/2   B. 1   C. 12   D. 24

5. Before the stirrup was invented, which of the following methods did people *not* use to mount their horses?
   A. Using a mounting sling   B. Training horses to drop to their knees
   C. Standing on a stool   D. Jumping on the horse's back

6. Which of the following can you *not* discover about a horse by looking into his mouth?
   A. Its age   B. Its sex
   C. A cause for weight loss   D. The breed of its father

71

Name: _____ Date: _____

Mammals: Horses (cont.)

7. If a female donkey mates with a male horse, the offspring is a:
   A.   Mule.   B.   Donkey.
   C.   Hinny.   D.   Jenny.

8. The V-shaped part of a horse's hoof is called the:
   A.   Sole.   B.   Shoe.
   C.   Frog.   D.   Nadir.

9. A horse sleeps:
   A.   Only lying down.   B.   Only standing up.
   C.   Either lying down or standing up.   D.   Only on its back.

10. What is a horse called before it reaches the age of one?
   A.   A yearling   B.   A weanling
   C.   A pony   D.   Seabicuit

11. How did the quarterhorse get its name?
   A.   It took four horses to pull a wagon.   B.   It was smaller than a regular horse.
   C.   From its speed in a quarter-mile race   D.   It was developed by José Quatro.

12. Horses can communicate how they are feeling by:
   A.   Facial expressions.   B.   The way they stand.
   C.   How they walk.   D.   The color of their eyes.

13. A horse's height is measured in:
   A.   Meters.   B.   Inches.
   C.   Feet.   D.   Hands.

14. How much weight loss does a racehorse average during a race?
   A.   Between 1 and 5 pounds   B.   Between 5 and 10 pounds
   C.   Between 15 and 25 pounds   D.   Between 20 and 55 pounds

15. If you were at a horse race, which horse would you bet on?
   A.   Nice Guy   B.   Bad News
   C.   Quitter   D.   January Molasses

16. The offspring of a horse and a zebra is called:
   A.   Zehorse.   B.   Horbra.
   C.   Mulinda.   D.   Golden zebra.

Mammals: Horses Answers

1. **B. January 1st.** By having all racehorses celebrate their birthdays on the same day, it makes it easier to group them together in age groups for races. Therefore, horse breeders plan to have a potential racehorse born as soon after the first of January as it is possible. This way, they will be more mature and stronger than those born later in the year. This will give them an advantage when they race against horses that are in their age group. These few extra months of development can be important when the horse begins racing as a two-year-old, although many do not begin racing until they are three or four years old.

2. **D. Firehouses have circular staircases.** Before there were fire engines, firetrucks were pulled by horses. These horses were kept on the ground floor but had a tendency to climb the straight staircases. They couldn't climb circular staircases, however. Even after horses were no longer used to pull firetrucks, circular staircases were still used because they took up less space than the traditional staircase.

3. **D. Riding.** Horses were around long before humans were. The first contact humans probably had with horses was to hunt them for food. Since horses were strong and fast, it was not a primary animal targeted for hunting. When first domesticated, horses were kept for their milk, meat, and skins. Some scientists now believe that the milk was the main reason for domesticating horses. Eventually these early farmers began moving from area to area and started using the horse as a pack animal. Then the farmers hitched the horse to a cart, enabling them to transport even more. Until this time, carts had been pulled by smaller, weaker animals. After that, people began riding horses.

4. **D. 24.** The term *horsepower* was invented by an engineer named James Watt who lived from 1736 to 1819. He is better-known for his work to improve the performance of steam engines. You also refer to him when you change a 100 "watt" light bulb. What is not as well known is that James Watt is the one who devised the method of measuring work done over time. He studied ponies working in mines and devised a measure of the amount of work they could do in a minute. Here is a simple way to describe horsepower: If a person were to lift 33,000 pounds one foot over a period of one minute, he would have been working at the rate of one horsepower. Scientists decided on the 24-horsepower figure based on a horse that weighed about 1,320 pounds.

5. **A. Using a mounting sling.** It was common for horses to be trained to kneel down like camels so they could be mounted.

6. **D. The breed of its father.** The sex of a horse can be determined by counting the teeth. Adult males horses generally have 40 teeth, while most females have 36. The age of a young horse can be accurately determined by examining the teeth as well. Horses' teeth grow for about six years, and each year after that, they wear down. Judging a horse's age by examining its teeth works best for horses that are not over ten years old. Weight loss is often caused by malnutrition. The most common cause of malnutrition or weight loss in old horses is tooth loss or dental damage. Their teeth may be completely worn out and damaged by years and years of grazing. Incidentally, a horse's teeth take up more room in its head than its brain does.

7. **C. Hinny.** When a male donkey and a female horse breed, they produce a mule. Hinnies and mules cannot breed with each other. A jenny is a female donkey.

8. **C. Frog.**

73

Mammals: Horses Answers (cont.)

9. **C. Either lying down or standing up.** Over time, horses developed an ability to sleep standing up in order to protect themselves from predators. If a horse sleeps while he is standing and is awakened by an approaching predator, the horse can get away a lot faster than if he were sleeping lying down. Horses are able to do this because they have a system of interlocking ligaments and bones in their legs, which acts as a sling that suspends their body weight without strain while their muscles are completely relaxed. Their legs are locked while they sleep and the horse doesn't have to use any energy to remain standing during sleep.

   However, horses don't sleep very deeply while they are standing. When they want a deep sleep, they will lie down. Horses use more energy lying down than they do when they are standing up.

10. **B. Weanling.** It remains a weanling until its first birthday, which is always on January 1. After January 1, it becomes a yearling.

11. **C. From its speed in a quarter-mile race.** This American breed of light horse originated during the colonial era, partly from the Arabian horse. The quarterhorse was named because the horse was able to run very fast for a quarter-mile. It is able to run faster than the thoroughbred for a short sprint. Quarterhorses were the most popular cattle horse in the early West, and today they are used for rodeo events.

12. **A. Facial expressions.** Horses use their ears, nostrils, and eyes to reveal their moods. A horse that flares its nostrils and puts its ears back is ready to attack.

13. **D. Hands.** One hand equals four inches.

14. **C. Between 15 and 25 pounds.**

15. **B. Bad News.** Bad news travels fast. Quitters never win. Nice guys finish last. Nothing is slower than molasses in January.

16. **D. Golden zebra.** Zebras are able to breed with other members of the horse family. A **zorse** is the offspring of a zebra stallion and a horse mare. Other terms seen are **zebroid, zony** or **zeony.** A cross between a zebra and donkey is called a **zebroid, zebrass, zonkey,** or **ze-donk.** Some people refer to any zebra hybrid as a "golden zebra."

Name: _____ Date: _____

Horse Idioms

Directions: An **idiom** is a figure of speech or an expression that is sometimes used to express an idea. Listed below is a group of expressions that use the word *horse*. Under each idiom, explain in your own words what the expression means.

1. Lock the barn door after the horse has gone. _____

_____

2. To get on one's high horse _____

_____

3. Change horses in midstream _____

_____

4. Put the cart before the horse _____

_____

5. Don't look a gift horse in the mouth. _____

_____

6. You can lead a horse to water, but you can't make it drink. _____

_____

7. Beating a dead horse _____

_____

8. Horse of a different color _____

_____

9. Hold your horses. _____

_____

10. Straight from the horse's mouth _____

_____

11. Eat like a horse _____

_____

12. Horse sense _____

_____

13. Horseplay _____

_____

14. A dark horse _____

_____

Name: _____ Date: _____

Farm Animals

Directions: Circle the letter of the correct answer(s). Not all of the questions in this quiz are about mammals.

1. The Blonde Mangalitza pig is a breed of pig in Hungary that has:
   A.   A snout longer than an elephant's.   B.   Fleece like a sheep.
   C.   Ears that are made into silk purses.   D.   Toes instead of hooves.

2. Which one of the following drinks is the most popular around the world?
   A.   Cow's milk   B.   Goat's milk
   C.   Donkey's milk   D.   Soy milk

3. Which of the following are donkeys *not* trained to do?
   A.   To guard sheep   B.   To provide rides at beaches
   C.   To participate in basketball games   D.   To help train dogs

4. Donkey's milk was once used as:
   A.   Medicine.   B.   Suntan lotion.
   C.   Furniture polish.   D.   A cure for baldness.

5. You can estimate a cow's age by the:
   A.   Shape of its teeth.   B.   Size of its teeth.
   C.   Color of its teeth.   D.   Number of rings on its horns.

6. Elderly cows in India have their own:
   A.   Health plan.   B.   Birthday parties.
   C.   Pets.   D.   Nursing homes.

7. On the top front of their mouth, cows have:
   A.   One wide tooth.   B.   Two teeth.
   C.   Four teeth.   D.   No teeth.

8. Which of the following products are *not* made from the bones, horns, hooves, blood, or gelatin of a cow?
   A.   Fire-extinguishing foam   B.   Film for cameras
   C.   China dishes   D.   Chess pieces

9. Which of the following products are *not* made from the fats and fatty acids of a cow?
   A.   Asphalt   B.   Lipstick
   C.   Eyeshadow   D.   Hydraulic brake fluid

10. Which of the following products are *not* made from the hide and hair of a cow?
    A.   Carpet cleaner   B.   Building insulation
    C.   Furniture   D.   Wallpaper

76

Name: _____   Date: _____

Farm Animals (cont.)

11. A cow has:
   A. One stomach.
   B. Two stomachs.
   C. Three stomachs.
   D. Four stomachs.

13. The collagen fibers found in the muscles of the intestines of sheep are used to make:
   A. Dogfood.
   B. Catfood.
   C. Tennis rackets.
   D. Quinine to treat malaria.

14. A two-year old sheep is called:
   A. A kid.
   B. A junior.
   C. A hogget.
   D. A two-tooth.

15. New Zealand sheep farmers must pay a tax on their sheep's:
   A. Wool.
   B. Weight.
   C. Gas.
   D. Sex.

16. Which of the following products are *not* made from pigs?
   A. Footballs
   B. Heart valves
   C. Cellophane
   D. Antifreeze

17. The chickens we buy at the grocery store are usually about:
   A. 5–8 weeks old.
   B. 3–5 months old.
   C. 6–9 months old
   D. 1–2 years old.

18. Farmers sometimes put what in a turkey's water and food in order to teach it to eat and drink?
   A. Sugar
   B. Salt
   C. Marbles
   D. Sawdust

19. A bull charges the cape of a bullfighter because:
   A. It is red.
   B. It is moving.
   C. It is large.
   D. Of its odor.

Farm Animals Answers

1. **B. Fleece like a sheep.** The Blonde Mangalitza pig, that has fleece like a sheep, is bred mainly to be turned into lard. There once was another type of pig that also had fleece like a sheep. It was called a Lincolnshire Curley Coat, but it is now extinct.

2. **B. Goat's milk.**

3. **D. To help train dogs.** Donkeys, or burros, are now being used by some ranchers and farmers to protect their sheep and goats. What makes donkeys so good at this job? They have natural herding instincts, and they dislike dogs and coyotes that prey on sheep. Mules are also used as guard animals, but not as much.

   Do donkeys play basketball? No, but they participate in "donkey basketball." There are companies that come into a community with a number of donkeys and arrange for a group of well-known people in the community to play donkey basketball. Tickets are sold, and the community group sponsoring the game receives some of the profits. Donkey basketball is similar to regular basketball except that players sit on top of donkeys during the whole game. Only players on donkeys are allowed to pass, throw, and shoot. While this kind of "sport" has been around for a long time, some critics say that it is cruel to donkeys who are frightened and often injured.

   Hundreds of donkeys provide rides on beaches in the United Kingdom. This tradition, which has been around since the nineteenth century, is strictly regulated by the government.

4. **A. Medicine.** Donkey's milk contains more protein and sugar but less fat than cow's milk. People used to think it could be used as a medicine and gave it to those who were sick and those who had tuberculosis. It was also fed to premature babies.

5. **D. The number of rings on its horns.**

6. **D. Nursing homes.** The world's 900 million believers of Hinduism respect animal life. Most people know that cows are considered holy in India, but so are other animals like elephants, mice, and monkeys.

7. **D. No teeth.** Cows have a total of 32 teeth. They have six molars on the top and bottom back and eight incisors on the bottom front. On the top front of their mouths, cows do not have any teeth; instead, they have a tough pad of skin.

8. **D. Chess pieces.** Other products made from the bones, horns, hooves, blood, and gelatin of a cow include Jell-O™, ice cream, and dogfood.

9. **C. Eyeshadow.** Other products made from the fats and fatty acids of a cow include candles, floor wax, tires, deodorant, bar soap, and shampoo. In addition, the pancreas of a cow is used to make insulin for diabetics, as well as other pharmaceutical products.

10. **A. Carpet cleaner.** Other products made from the hide and hair of the cow include paint brushes, building insulation, wallpaper, furniture glue, tennis shoes, leather jackets, belts, suede, baseballs, baseball gloves, and soccer balls.

11. **A. One stomach.** Many believe that a cow has four stomachs. Actually, it has one stomach with four compartments. This enables a cow to eat things other animals can't. The food goes into compartment one and is softened. When the food goes into compartment two, it mixes

Farm Animals Answers (cont.)

and softens more and develops into a material called "cud." When the cow is full, it burps up some of the cud to chew it again. It may chew the cud for eight hours each day. After chewing the cud, the cow swallows again, and the cud passes into the third and fourth compartments where further digestion takes place. It then goes to the intestines where the nutrients are absorbed. A typical cow will chew about 50 times per minute. In one day, a cow moves its jaw more than 40,000 times.

13. **C. Tennis rackets.** Gut strings for tennis rackets are made from the intestines of sheep, horses, cows, or pigs. These strings are more fragile than synthetic strings and can be damaged by moisture or high humidity. Gut strings are not as elastic as synthetic strings so players are able to return the ball at a much higher speed. Most rackets now use synthetic strings. Quinine is a drug that is made from the bark of the cinchona tree.

14. **D. A two-tooth**. Sheep grow two teeth a year until they have eight. A one-year old sheep is called a hogget. They only have lower teeth that press against an upper palette.

15. **C. Gas.** New Zealand sheep farmers must pay a tax on the methane emissions of their sheep. Experts tell us that the icecaps are melting, and they blame much of the problem on the greenhouse effect caused by gases. Carbon dioxide is the most common greenhouse gas in the world and is caused by burning fossil fuels such as coal, oil, and gas, but methane gas also contributes to the problem, and it comes from livestock. So New Zealand, which is a world leader for sheep and beef production, decided to tax ranchers on the number of cattle, sheep, and deer they own. This is called a "flatulence" tax. The more animals they keep, the higher their tax.

16. **A. Footballs.** Even though footballs are referred to as pigskins, today's footballs are made from cowskins. It takes about 3,000 cows to supply the National Football League with enough leather for a year's supply of footballs. Other products that depend on the bones and skin of pigs include shoes, gloves, buttons, bone china, and glue. A pig's hair is used to make upholstery, brushes for artists, and insulation. The fatty acids and glycerin in pigs are used in the production of weedkillers, insecticides, cosmetics, chalk, floor waxes, waterproofing agents, cement, rubber, crayons, antifreeze, plastics, putty, and cellophane. Many drugs, including insulin, come from pigs. Diseased heart valves in humans are often replaced with healthy valves from pigs.

17. **A. 5–8 weeks old.** Once chickens are large enough to slaughter and sell, it doesn't make much sense to keep feeding and taking care of them. Humans eat about eight billion chickens per year. If all the chickens KFC™ serves each year were laid out toe-to-beak, they would circle the earth more than ten times.

18. **C. Marbles.** Turkeys are not very smart. They need to be taught to eat and drink. Farmers put marbles in their water and feed. The turkeys peck at the shiny marbles, and as their beaks slide off the marbles, they get food and water. After a few days, the turkeys no longer need the marbles.

19. **B. It is moving.** Bulls are colorblind, so it is not the red color that angers the bull but the movement that they find irritating.

Name: _____ Date: _____

Farm Animal Idioms

Directions: An **idiom** is a figure of speech or an expression that is sometimes used to express an idea. Listed below is a group of expressions that uses the names of farm animals. Under each idiom, explain in your own words what the expression means.

1. Take the bull by the horns.

   _____

   _____

2. A sacred cow _____

3. Like a bull in a china shop _____

   _____

4. Like a red cape to a bull _____

   _____

5. Hit the bull's-eye. _____

   _____

6. Bullheaded _____

   _____

7. Till the cows come home _____

   _____

8. A cash cow _____

   _____

9. To kill the goose that lays the golden egg _____

   _____

10. A scapegoat _____

    _____

11. Get your goat _____

    _____

12. In two shakes of a lamb's tail _____

    _____

Name: _____ Date: _____

Farm Animal Idioms (cont.)

13. Separate the sheep from the goats _____

_____

14. Chicken feed _____

_____

15. To run around like a chicken with its head cut off _____

_____

16. Chickens come home to roost _____

_____

17. Don't count your chickens before they are hatched. _____

_____

18. Go to bed with the chickens _____

_____

19. To chicken out _____

_____

20. A sitting duck _____

_____

21. To get all of one's ducks in a row _____

_____

22. Like water off a duck's back _____

_____

23. Take to it like a duck to water _____

_____

24. A cock-and-bull story _____

_____

25. A wild goose chase _____

_____

Name: _____   Date: _____

Top border (left to right): N O A N C T N U O B S

Left border (top to bottom): T L D E O A W D N A

Right border (top to bottom): S R R E I P A A T H S

Bottom border (left to right): S C T O A W I U R P S

Cow Puzzle

Throughout history, cattle have been important to humans. Cattle have provided meat, milk, leather, glue, gelatin, and other products. There are two species of modern cattle. One originated in Europe and is the kind that we use for beef and milk. The other originated in India. It is mostly found in Africa and Asia. Historians say that European cattle probably are descended from wild cattle, which were first domesticated in Europe about 8,500 years ago. In addition to providing meat and milk, cattle were also used to pull carts, for sport, and for sacrifice. The male of the species is called a bull. The female is a cow. The young cow is called a calf. A heifer is a female that has not given birth.

An interesting fact about cows is hidden in the frame around the picture of the cow shown above. To discover this fact, you must go around the frame twice, reading every *other* letter. Where do you start, and which way do you read around the frame? That's what you have to figure out.

Answer: _____

_____

Name: _____ Date: _____

Mammals: Bats

There are many species of bats living on every continent except Antarctica. Each species has adapted to its environment and has adjusted its diet for where it lives. Almost all of the bats in the world eat insects, and many use **echolocation** in order to find food and fly in the dark. Many of those who eat insects can consume up to 2,000 mosquito-sized insects in one night. These bats need to eat so much because they use a lot of energy to fly. Some bats have developed very good eyesight as well as a keen sense of smell that is needed to find ripe fruit. Species that live in the desert and eat nectar have developed the long tongues and noses necessary to extract the nectar from flowers. There are some bats that eat small animals. They have developed claws for catching their prey and sharp teeth with which to eat them. There are a few bats living in Latin America that only eat blood.

People often fear bats. This might be because they feed at night, they are secretive, and are not often seen. So some people think that bats are dangerous, dirty, bloodsuckers and carriers of disease. For the most part, these fears are unfounded. Bats are mammals that benefit humans. They help to control night-flying insects, pollinate plants, and scatter the seeds of plants. Their guano (droppings) is rich in nitrogen and has been sold as fertilizer. Rather than harming people, bats do their best to avoid contact with humans.

Directions: Circle the letter of the correct answer(s).

1. The saliva of vampire bats is being studied as:
   A. A treatment for stroke.
   C. Insect repellent.
   B. A super glue.
   D. Insect bait.

2. Bats are the only mammals that:
   A. Use echolocation to "see."
   C. Eat insects.
   B. Feed at night.
   D. Can fly.

3. What happens if vampire bats can't eat blood for two straight nights?
   A. They die.
   C. They will eat small amphibians.
   B. They will eat insects.
   D. They will eat fish.

4. Which of the following is true?
   A. Bats are birds.
   C. Bats are blind.
   B. Bats tangle themselves in human hair.
   D. Bats rarely give humans disease.

5. Vampire bats are the only known mammals that:
   A. Originated in Transylvania.
   C. Lay eggs.
   B. Survive solely on blood.
   D. Hunt at night.

Name: _____ Date: _____

Mammals: Bats (cont.)

6. There are about _____ different species of bats in the world.
   A. 10
   B. 100
   C. 1,000
   D. 10,000

7. In Africa, small woolly bats sleep in:
   A. Their mother's arms.
   B. Spider webs.
   C. Church towers.
   D. Lions' dens.

8. The largest bat in the world is the:
   A. 727.
   B. Big Bertha.
   C. Flying fox.
   D. Gargantua.

9. The world's smallest bat is the Kitti's hog-nosed bat, also known as the bumblebee bat. It weighs:
   A. One ounce.
   B. Two ounces.
   C. Two grams.
   D. One gram.

10. Besides man, bats are the only mammals that:
    A. Carry their lunches with them.
    B. "Teach" their young.
    C. Choose food because of its taste.
    D. Choose a mate because of appearance.

11. If a bat is awakened during hibernation, it may:
    A. Die.
    B. Migrate.
    C. Fly to a new roost.
    D. Sleep well into summer.

12. The short-nosed bat is one of the few bats that makes:
    A. Wine.
    B. Bread.
    C. Nests.
    D. Tents to live in.

13. The greater bamboo bat lives:
    A. Underground.
    B. In Bamboo, China.
    C. Inside bamboo stems.
    D. With pythons.

14. Without its thumbs, the vampire bat might not be able to:
    A. Find a mate.
    B. Fly.
    C. Hitchhike home.
    D. Catch its prey.

15. Well-fed vampire bats will often trade what for grooming?
    A. A roost
    B. A mate
    C. Regurgitated blood
    D. A baby bat

Mammals: Bats Answers

1. **A. A treatment for stroke.** A stroke is sometimes called a "brain attack," and happens when part of the brain is deprived of oxygen because of a clogged artery or burst blood vessel. Without oxygen, the brain and nerve cells can suffer permanent damage. So what does this have to do with a vampire bat? With their sharp teeth, vampire bats make small cuts in the skin of a sleeping animal. A chemical in their saliva numbs the animal's skin and prevents them from waking up. Another chemical in the bat's saliva contains a substance that keeps the blood from clotting. The bats are then able to lap up the blood that oozes from the wound. Scientists are studying the chemical that prevents clotting to see if it would work in stroke victims to dissolve the clot causing the stroke. Initial studies on mice showed that the chemical from the vampire bat saliva was able to be used up to three times longer than the current stroke treatment and without additional risk for brain damage side effects.

2. **D. Can fly.** People used to think bats were birds. But since they do not have feathers, they are not birds. Bats are mammals, and like all mammals, they are warmblooded, nurse their young, and have fur. They are the only mammals that flap their wings and can fly. You may have heard of flying squirrels, which are mammals too, but they don't really flap their wings and fly. They glide. They jump from one branch to another, stretch out, and glide to a lower branch.

   Toothed whales, which are also mammals and not fish, also use **echolocation**. They emit sounds that bounce off objects.

   Many mammals are **insectivores**, which means that they eat insects. Some other mammals that eat insects are aardvarks, anteaters, moles, and shrews. Other animals are **carnivores**, which means they eat the flesh of animals. Others are **herbivores**, which means they eat plants. There are also **omnivores**, which eat both plants and the flesh of animals.

3. **A. They die.**

4. **D. Bats rarely give humans disease.** It is a myth that bats are blind, become entangled in human hair, and transmit diseases to other animals or humans. Fruit bats have larger eyes than insect-eating bats who use echolocation to find their food. But bats can see, and many species have vision that is especially good at night when they hunt. While all mammals can get rabies, less than one-half of one percent of bats do, and they usually only bite someone in self defense. So if you do not pick up a bat, there is little chance you will be infected. Rabies from bats claims only one human death per year in the United States.

5. **B. Survive solely on blood.**

6. **C. 1,000.** Bats live all over the world, except for the coldest parts. Bats make up one-fifth of the world's mammals. They are the second-largest group of mammals. Rodents are the largest group.

7. **B. Spider webs.**

8. **C. Flying fox.** Flying foxes roost (rest or sleep) outside in the sun rather than in caves, as many bats do. Flying foxes hang upside down together in colonies, also called "camps" with as many as a million others. Flying foxes are **frugivores**, which means they eat fruit. They also eat flowers and pollen and pollinate flowers in the same way bees do. They have wingspans of over six feet and weigh about two pounds.

9. **C. Two grams.** The bumblebee bat comes from Thailand and Myanmar (Burma). It lives in limestone caves and eats insects. It was discovered in 1974 and is on the list of endangered species.

Mammals: Bats Answers (cont.)

10. **A. Carry their lunches with them.** A bat makes a pouch by curling its tail and fills it with insects so that it can eat as it flies.

11. **A. Die.** When winter approaches and insects are no longer available, a bat will either migrate or hibernate. It has accumulated a layer of fat that will sustain it through the winter no matter what it does. A bat may migrate as long a distance as 1,000 miles. Or it may hibernate in a cave or in some other remote roost. When a bat hibernates, it uses up stored energy very slowly. When it wakes up in the winter, it uses energy faster and may starve to death because there is no food for it at this time of the year. Also, once awakened, a bat may decide to move to another site, and when it does, it uses even more energy. If a bat is disturbed two or three times during the winter, it can burn up all its energy reserves and die. When bats are disturbed during the winter, they may leave their young, and that will cause the young to die also.

12. **D. Tents to live in.** There aren't many safe places for a small bat to roost in a forest. While larger bats that eat fruit can fly long distances to a safe cave, smaller bats can't do this. So in order to protect themselves and still live close to their food source, they make tents out of leaves. The bats will choose large-leafed plants such as palms or bananas and then chew the leaf veins so the leaf collapses to form a tent. When their food supply runs out in a certain area, they leave and make a tent in another location.

13. **C. Inside bamboo stems.** There are a few bats that live under tree bark. The greater bamboo bat roosts inside hollow bamboo stems. The New Zealand short-tailed bat roosts in tree hollows that it may dig with its teeth.

14. **B. Fly.** The vampire bat drinks more than its own weight in blood every night. After feeding, it has added so much body weight that in order for it to fly, it uses its long thumbs to push itself up into the air.

15. **C. Regurgitated blood.**

Name: _____ Date: _____

Mythbuster: Bats

Directions: Shown on the following page are a number of questions and statements concerning bats. Fill in the spaces below with the correct word that goes with the statement. Then take the letters in the circle and put them in the spaces below the puzzle. The words that are spelled from these letters explain a myth about bats.

1.

2.

3.

4.

5.

6.

7.

8.

9.

10.

11.

12.

13.

14.

15.

ANSWER: ___ ___ ___   ___ ___ ___ ___ ___   ___ ___ ___ ___ ___ .

Name: _____   Date: _____

Mythbuster: Bats (cont.)

1.   This bat is the world's smallest mammal.

2.   This a group of animals that is covered with hair or fur and feeds its young milk. Most give birth to live babies.

3.   Bats use sound in order to navigate in the dark. This process of using ultra-high frequency sounds is called _____.

4.   Bats are able to sleep upside down because of their strong _____.

5.   Bats are not birds because they have fur instead of these.

6.   People are afraid that bats may give them this disease.

7.   Bats sometimes pollinate flowers, just as these insects do.

8.   Most bats eat these creatures.

9.   This is a place where bats rest.

10.   This is the only continent where bats do not live.

11.   During the cold months, some bats migrate, and others do this.

12.   One of the main groups of animals upon which vampire bats feed in South and Central America is _____.

13.   This ability is what separates bats from other mammals.

14.   This is the time that bats prefer to fly.

15.   This is what vampire bats find nourishing.

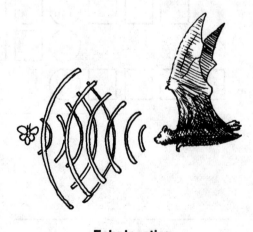

Echolocation

Name: _____ Date: _____

Mammals: Sea Creatures—Whales

Whales are not fish. Whales, porpoises, and dolphins are called **cetaceans**. Cetaceans are **mammals** that live in the sea. They are warmblooded, have hair, breathe air, and bear young who drink their mother's milk. Whales live in every ocean from the poles to the tropics. They come in all sizes from the blue whale that weighs up to 150 tons and is 100 feet in length to several small whales that weigh less than 100 pounds and are about 3 feet long.

There are two kinds of whales, **toothed whales** and **baleen whales**. Toothed whales, such as the sperm whale, have teeth and eat squid and fish. Baleen whales, such as the huge blue whale, eat by straining food, like krill or fish, from the water. Krill are shrimp-like marine animals. The toothed whale has one blowhole, a nostril, while the baleen whale has two.

Directions: Circle the letter of the correct answer(s).

1. What is the world's largest living fish?
   A.   Blue whale   B.   Mauve whale   C.   Sailfish   D.   Whale shark

2. When blue whales are first born, they gain as much as:
   A.   20 pounds a day.   B.   100 pounds a day.
   C.   200 pounds a day.   D.   1,000 pounds a day.

3. What are the largest animals to have ever lived?
   A.   Dinosaurs   B.   Blue whales   C.   Mastodons   D.   Giraffes

4. What is the loudest animal?
   A.   Howler monkey   B.   Blue whale   C.   Shrieking whale   D.   Football coach

5. Until 1973, whale oil was used in some:
   A.   Car transmissions.   B.   Vitamins.
   C.   Artists' paints.   D.   Manufacturing of plastic.

6. The gray whale is believed to have:
   A.   Dark pink skin.   B.   The longest flippers of any whale.
   C.   The most complex mating call.   D.   The longest migration of any mammal.

7. Killer whales along the South American coast spend a lot of their time:
   A.   Eating coconuts.   B.   Surfing.
   C.   Playing with penguins.   D.   Attacking swimmers.

8. A sperm whale uses what to stun its victims?
   A.   Sound   B.   Smell
   C.   Light   D.   Electricity

9. The blue whale's sound is so deep and powerful that the sound can travel underwater:
   A.   For a mile.   B.   For ten miles.
   C.   For one hundred miles.   D.   For one thousand miles.

Name: _____   Date: _____

Mammals: Sea Creatures—Whales (cont.)

10. Before a whale is born, it has:
    A.   A thick coat of curly hair.   B.   A beard.
    C.   Hands and fingers.   D.   Scales.

11. Southern right whales have been seen to raise their flukes (the lobes of their tails) and:
    A.   Kill a seal.   B.   Use them as sails.
    C.   Wave at sailors.   D.   Swat at birds.

12. The Latin name for the blue whale is *Balaenoptera musculus*. The word *musculus* means:
    A.   Winged mouse.   B.   Large.   C.   Sea king.   D.   Blue.

13. When feeding, each mouthful of water that an adult blue whale takes in to trap its prey contains:
    A.   100 gallons of water.   B.   1,000 gallons of water.
    C.   10,000 gallons of water.   D.   100,000 gallons of water.

14. Ambergris is a waxy substance that is often found floating in tropical waters. It comes from the intestine of the sperm whale. For which of the following has ambergris *not* been used to manufacture?
    A.   Perfume   B.   Earplugs
    C.   Spice   D.   Medicine

15. When a whale sleeps, it:
    A.   Rests one-half of its brain.   B.   Snores.
    C.   Lies on its back.   D.   Hums.

16. The whale with the longest lifespan is the bowhead whale. One was reported to have lived:
    A.   57 years.   B.   130 years.   C.   187 years.   D.   317 years.

17. Beluga whales are sometimes called:
    A.   Killers of the sea.   B.   Sea canaries.
    C.   Sea pilots.   D.   Ocean ghosts.

18. Many years ago, sailors thought the narwhal was related to the:
    A.   Porpoise.   B.   Seal.   C.   Unicorn.   D.   Mermaid.

19. In the 1970s, a group of humpback whales did something that no other group of whales had ever done before. They:
    A.   Kept a drowning child afloat.   B.   Guided a rescue ship to a shipwreck.
    C.   Brought a sick whale to a veterinarian.   D.   Had a hit record.

90

Name: _____ Date: _____

Mammals: Sea Creatures—Whales (cont.)

20. When a female sperm whale dives for food, her calf:
    A. Dives with her.   B. Is watched by a babysitter.
    C. Is given a toy to play with.   D. Is left alone.

21. Killer whales:
    A. Kill more than ten humans a year.   B. Only eat krill.
    C. Cannot live in captivity.   D. Are related to dolphins.

22. When orcas (killer whales) are traveling in groups, they
    A. Attack smaller whales.   B. Swim only at night.
    C. Breathe in unison.   D. Never eat.

23. The sperm whale family pod is directed by:
    A. The largest male.   B. The smartest male.
    C. The largest female.   D. A pilot whale.

24. Humpback whales catch their fish by:
    A. Using smaller fish as bait.   B. Stealing them from other whales.
    C. Pretending to be dead.   D. Using a net of bubbles.

25. When the humpback whale sings, it:
    A. Hangs upside down.   B. Puts its head out of the water.
    C. Goes to the bottom of the ocean.   D. Keeps time with its flipper.

26. Years ago, whalers would call a blue whale:
    A. Big blue.   B. Sulphur bottom.   C. Blue ghost.   D. Larry.

27. Whenever a male humpback whale finds a female, it will:
    A. Sing and blow bubbles.   B. Dance and wave.
    C. Spin and dive.   D. Shake and burp.

28. Located inside a whale's tail are many tiny blood vessels that:
    A. Keep it cool.   B. Keep it upright.
    C. Help it find food.   D. Warn of a predator.

29. Which of the following statements concerning the head of a sperm whale is *not* true?
    A. It contains the largest of all brains.   B. It is full of oil.
    C. It extends over 50 percent of its body. D. It has two blowholes.

30. Each day a blue whale eats up to how many ton(s) of krill?
    A. One ton   B. Two tons   C. Three tons   D. Four tons

91

Mammals: Sea Creatures—Whales Answers

1. **B. Whale shark.** The whale shark can grow to be 50 feet long. It is a filter feeder that takes in enormous amounts of plankton to eat as it swims. It has about 300 rows of teeth, with hundreds of small teeth in each row. The second biggest fish in the ocean is the basking shark, which grows to be about 40 feet long. It is also a filter feeder.

2. **C. 200 pounds a day.** A newborn blue whale calf can weigh close to three tons and measure 23 feet in length. A blue whale calf drinks about 130 gallons of fat-rich mother's milk each day, and gains up to 200 pounds per day during its nursing period—that's eight to ten pounds an hour. At about eight months of age, when the calf stops drinking its mother's milk, it may weigh 50,000 pounds and be 50 feet long. A blue whale calf can swim 22 miles per hour.

3. **B. Blue whales.** The blue whale is a species of baleen whale that weighs approximately 130 tons and may attain a length of more than 98 feet. Its weight is about the same as four of the largest dinosaurs, or 24 elephants, or 1,500 men. A blue whale's tongue alone is about the size and weight of an African elephant. It is so large that fifty people could stand on it. Its heart is about the size of a Volkswagen Beetle car and weighs about 1,500 pounds. The spout from its blowhole can reach almost 30 feet high. Females are generally larger than males. They spend the summer in polar waters eating krill, which are shrimp-like crustaceans. A blue whale may eat up to four tons of krill a day. In the winter, blue whales move toward the equator to breed. A newborn baby blue whale is the size of a full-grown elephant.

4. **B. Blue whale.** The blue whale is the loudest animal on Earth. The sound made by a blue whale is louder than the roar of a rocket or the sound of heavy gunfire. Its sound is as loud as 188 decibels.

5. **A. Car transmissions.**

6. **D. The longest migration of any mammal.** Each year along the Pacific Coast, gray whales participate in their annual migration. They will travel back and forth between the Arctic and Baja California. Some travel even farther south than that. The round trip is between 10,000 and 12,000 miles. First in the procession are the pregnant females who need to feed and nourish not only themselves, but their developing fetuses. Next, the nonbreeding females and the adult males. The smaller, younger whales are next in the procession, and the final group that travel to the feeding grounds are the mothers and calves.

7. **B. Surfing.** Killer whales along the South American coast do surf. They will ride in on a wave and grab a sea lion off of the beach. Then the whales work their way back out to sea on the next wave. Once it catches the sea lion, the adult will play with it by tossing it high into the air. This is not the only place where whales go to play with their prey. Off the coast of Africa, killer whales catch penguins and cormorants. They will grab birds with their mouths and then release them.

8. **A. Sound.** Sperm whales use **echolocation** in order to locate their prey. Echolocation is the system some animals use in order to locate distant or invisible objects by using sound waves that are reflected back by objects or prey. This is the same method bats use to fly at night. Sperm whales are not only able to locate their prey with the loud noises they make, but the pressure waves created by the sound stun their victim. Once the victim is stunned, the whale scoops it up with its mouth.

9. **D. For a thousand miles.**

92

Mammals: Sea Creatures—Whales Answers (cont.)

10. **C. Hands and fingers.** Whale fetuses have hands and fingers, which fuse together before they are born.

11. **B. Use them as sails.** Mariners have reported they have seen southern right whales raise their flukes in the wind and use them as sails.

12. **A. Winged mouse.** The Latin name for the blue whale is *Balaenoptera musculus.* "Musculus" means "winged mouse." Carolus Linnaeus, a Swedish botanist and explorer, was the first to develop the principles for defining organisms and creating a system for naming them. In 1758, as a joke, Linnaeus named the blue whale the "winged mouse."

13. **D. 10,000 gallons of water.** There are up to 10,000 gallons of water in each feeding mouthful of an adult blue whale. That would be equal to 256,000 glasses of water. Of course, they don't swallow that salt water; they use their baleen to strain it out.

14. **B. Earplugs.** Ambergris is a waxy substance that floats and washes ashore. While fresh ambergris is black and soft and has a foul odor, it becomes hard and turns yellow or gray and has a pleasant smell after it has been exposed to the sun and air. In some cultures, ambergris was used for medicines and as a spice. It has also been used to stabilize the scent of expensive perfumes and to keep the scent from evaporating. However, ambergris is hardly ever used today because of trade restrictions. Synthetically produced chemicals are now used to accomplish the same things for which ambergris was once used.

15. **A. Rests one-half of its brain.** Whales do not sleep in the same way in which humans do. If they did, they might die. Humans breathe involuntarily. This means that we do not have to think about breathing. We just do it naturally. We breathe when we are asleep and even when we are unconscious. This is not true of whales. Whales are voluntary breathers. This means that they do not breathe unless they think about it. So how do they sleep and think about breathing at the same time? Scientists believe the whale accomplishes this by using a process called **unihemispherical sleep**. This simply means that the whale is able to sleep and rest one-half of its brain, while the other half of the brain remains awake, or active, so it can remember to breathe.

16. **B. 130 years.**

17. **B. Sea canaries**. They are called "sea canaries" because their songs sound like canaries singing.

18. **C. Unicorn.** The narwhal, which is sometimes spelled *narwhale*, is a small, toothed whale that lives along coasts and in the rivers of the Arctic. The male narwhal has a long, straight tusk that protrudes from above the mouth. The tusk is more than three feet long and is grooved into a spiral shape. Although many people describe the tusk of a narwhal as a horn, it is actually one of the narwhal's teeth. The narwhal has two teeth, but usually only the left tooth of the male develops into a tusk. This tusk was thought to look like the mythical unicorn's horn. Sailors who found one of these tusks would often sell it by telling the buyer that it was from a unicorn and that it had magical powers.

19. **D. Had a hit record**. Sailors and whalers have always said that whales make sounds, but scientists did not believe them because when they examined whales, they found no vocal cords. They believed that whales were incapable of making sounds. They know today, however, that whales are not only capable of making sounds, they are able to compose and sing very elaborate songs. How they accomplish this is still debated by scientists.

In the early 1950s, military personnel were listening for enemy submarines under the water

Mammals: Sea Creatures—Whales Answers (cont.)

when they recorded a series of unusual sounds that they could not identify. The sounds were different from anything they had ever heard before. There was grunting, clicking, moaning, squealing, wailing, and screeching. While these sounds might not be considered unusual, what was unusual was that they were made in a pattern that was repeated over and over. Eventually, it was learned that the sounds were coming from whales. The sounds were labeled "songs" because they were individual sounds of different frequencies that were made in a certain order, just like a song.

While many different species of whales sing, the most complicated and unusual songs are composed by humpback whales. The humpback whale hangs upside down in the water and sings all day long. Its song may be only a few minutes long or may be as long as 30 minutes. When the humpback finishes its song, it stops for a few minutes and then goes back to the beginning and sings the same song all over again. All of the whales in the same area will sing similar songs. Individual whales copy parts of a song from other whales, and, over a period of years, the song will change. Humpbacks in other parts of the world sing a different song. While scientists can't be sure of the purpose of the songs, it is believed that the songs are used to attract females and to warn other males to stay away. They may also be used for identification or to aid in their annual migration.

In the 1970s, humpback songs were recorded, and their record became a hit on the pop music charts. Humpback whales not only had a hit record, but their recordings were put onboard the *Voyager* space probe and sent into outer space.

20. **B. Is watched by a babysitter.** Researchers believe that the sperm whale dives deeper than any other whale. In one study, it was shown that sperm whales can dive as deep as two miles and are capable of holding their breath for two hours. When a mother dives for food, her calf is watched by another female until she returns.

21. **D. Are related to dolphins.** There are no records of humans attacked by killer whales.

22. **C. Breathe in unison.**

23. **C. The largest female.** Sperm whales have a matriarchal society. This means the pod (a group of whales) is guided and directed by a large female. In some cases, the leader gets sick and beaches herself on shore. When this happens, the others often follow because they are used to following their leader.

24. **D. Using a net of bubbles.** A humpback whale first blows a net of bubbles around a school of fish. This confuses the fish, and then the whale swims up through the bubble net to catch its food.

25. **A. Hangs upside down.**

26. **B. Sulphur bottom.** Whalers gave the blue whale this name because of the algae growing on the belly of the blue whale, which made the belly appear yellow—the same color of sulfur.

27. **A. Sing and blow bubbles.**

28. **A. Keep it cool.** In fact, some people say that this acts like the radiator of a car.

29. **D. It has two blowholes.** A sperm whale is the largest, toothed whale. It can be almost 60 feet long and weigh almost 50 tons. Its head extends over half the length of its body. A sperm whale has the largest brain that has ever existed. It contains a waxy substance known as spermaceti oil.

30. **D. Four tons.** This is the same as eating a fully grown African elephant every day.

94

Name: _____ Date: _____

Mammals: Sea Creatures—Sea Otters

Sea otters are a marine species that usually lives in kelp beds. The sea otter's fur is very thick and varies in color from brown to reddish. Its hind feet are large and shaped like flippers, while its forefeet are smaller. Sea otters spend a great deal of time on their backs. They rest, sleep, and often swim on their backs. There are two populations of sea otters that live in North America. One is the Alaska sea otter, and the other is the California sea otter. California sea otters are usually about four feet in length. The males weigh about 65 pounds, while the females average around 45 pounds. California sea otters spend almost all of their time in the water. This contrasts with the Alaska sea otters that often sleep, groom, and nurse on land. Alaska sea otters are larger than the California sea otters and can reach up to 100 pounds. Before the sea otter was protected, it was hunted almost to extinction by 1910. Its numbers have stabilized and are now increasing.

Directions: Circle the letter of the correct answer(s).

1. A sea otter's skin:
   A. Never gets wet.
   C. Has no fur.
   B. Can be used as sandpaper.
   D. Is used as a flotation device.

2. A sea otter is one of the few animals that:
   A. Gets permission to eat from the leader.
   C. Uses a tool.
   B. Feeds its children first.
   D. Washes its food.

3. Next to eating, the sea otter spends most of its time:
   A. Playing.
   C. Looking for a mate.
   B. Grooming its fur.
   D. Looking for sand dollars.

4. In order to avoid being swept out to sea while they sleep, sea otters:
   A. Only sleep in a rip current.
   C. Go ashore.
   B. Take turns being on watch.
   D. Tie themselves together.

5. When a mother sea otter dives for food, she leaves her pup:
   A. With a babysitter.   B. Tied up.   C. With her mate.   D. On a rock.

6. Sea otters are members of the:
   A. Seal family.   B. Manatee family.   C. Dolphin family.   D. Weasel family.

7. The sea otter stays warm because:
   A. It has blubber.
   C. It has two coats of fur.
   B. It forms a ball with other otters.
   D. It keeps moving.

8. Which of the following are *not* responsible for the decline of the sea otter's population?
   A. Sea urchin
   C. Salmon gill nets
   B. Oil
   D. Eagles

95

Mammals: Sea Creatures—Sea Otters Answers

1. **A. Never gets wet.** The sea otter's fur is very fine and dense. A large male animal may have up to 650,000 hairs per square inch. This fur is dense for a very important reason. The sea otter doesn't have blubber as other marine mammals do. It needs thick, dense fur in order to keep warm. There are oils in a sea otter's fur that repel water so that, in spite of the fact that the sea otter lives in the ocean, its skin stays dry. In addition, the thick fur traps small air bubbles so there is a layer of warm air between the otter's skin and the cold water and air.

2. **C. Uses a tool.** The sea otter from the Pacific coast of North America dives to the seabed in order to collect its meal of crabs, clams, and other shelled creatures. While on the bottom, it also picks up a stone. When it returns to the surface, the otter rolls over on its back, floats, and puts the stone on its chest. It then uses the stone like an anvil. It holds the shellfish in its front paws and slams it against the stone until it breaks open so it can eat the contents. Once it finds a stone that works well, the otter may use it over and over. A sea otter also dives while holding the stone under its armpit and uses the stone as a hammer underneath the water to smash abalone (a shellfish) that is attached to the bottom of the ocean.

3. **B. Grooming its fur.** Up to 48 percent of the sea otter's daylight hours are spent grooming its fur. It grooms by rubbing its fur with its forepaws. Using its strong claws as combs, it rakes through its fur and rubs it with its forepaws. The sea otter then twirls around in the water to smooth its fur down. One of the hazards sea otters have had to deal with over the past few years is oil spills. If an otter gets oil on its fur, the insulating qualities of the fur are lost. Water will penetrate the fur, the skin becomes wet, and the sea otter may die from the cold.

4. **D. Tie themselves together.** Groups of sea otters frequently entangle themselves in beds of seaweed as the sun sets. They actually become a large raft that will stay together until the sun rises. At other times, sea otters may wrap themselves in kelp while eating and resting.

5. **B. Tied up.** Sea otter pups spend their first eight months with their mothers. The mothers carry them on their chests and groom them often. When they are about four weeks old, the pups begin to learn how to swim. A pup is unable to dive underwater because its fur traps so much air. When a mother sea otter dives to get food, she does not have to worry about the pup drowning, but she does worry that it might drift away, so she wraps it in kelp for safekeeping. It stays there bobbing like a cork until she returns.

6. **D. Weasel family.** The weasel family is closely related to the mink and river otters. Their webbed hind feet are well-adapted for swimming, since otters spend most of their time in the water. Sea otters stay in or near the water because they are very clumsy on land.

7. **C. It has two coats of fur.**

8. **A. Sea urchin.** Illegal shooting of sea otters by fishermen, as well as the legal hunting of otters by indigenous peoples, are the main causes of the decline in the otter population. Salmon gill nets, oil, brown bears, and eagles are other causes. If an otter's fur gets coated with oil or any other substance, it loses its insulating ability, and the otter can die from cold and exposure. The sea otter feeds on sea urchins, among other things.

Name: _____ Date: _____

Mammals: Sea Creatures—Dolphins

Dolphins are toothed whales closely related to the killer whale and pilot whale. Most of them are small, less than ten feet long. Dolphins are graceful, smart, friendly, and playful. The bottlenose dolphin looks like it is smiling because of the way its mouth is shaped. Dolphins are occasionally called porpoises, but porpoises are usually smaller than dolphins and have rounded, cone-shaped heads and do not have the dolphin's characteristic beak.

Directions: Circle the letter of the correct answer(s).

1. A dolphin can be recognized by its:
   A.   Eyes.   B.   Dorsal fin.   C.   Face.   D.   Flippers.

2. When a dolphin sleeps, it:
   A.   Keeps one eye open.   B.   Makes a hammock of kelp.
   C.   Only sleeps one minute at a time.   D.   Sings.

3. Dolphins have been known to:
   A.   Wear makeup.   B.   Disguise themselves with kelp.
   C.   Play practical jokes.   D.   Have marriage ceremonies.

4. Which of the following body parts do dolphins use to hear?
   A.   Ear holes   B.   Head   C.   Bones in their ears   D.   Jawbone

5. Dolphins find their food in the same way as:
   A.   Bats.   B.   Squids.   C.   Sharks.   D.   Dingos.

6. Bottlenose dolphins swim in groups called:
   A.   Herds.   B.   Pods.   C.   Flocks.   D.   Prides.

7. Compared to the human brain, the brain of a bottlenose dolphin is:
   A.   Smaller.   B.   Larger.   C.   The same size.   D.   More intelligent.

8. If a baby dolphin swims too far away from its mother, the mother may:
   A.   Give the baby a time out.   B.   Spank the baby.
   C.   Abandon the baby.   D.   Bite the baby.

9. The Amazon river dolphin is unusual because it:
   A.   Is pink.   B.   Is the size of a guppy.
   C.   Eats monkeys.   D.   Has a thick coat of hair.

10. The navy refers to dolphins as:
    A.   Flippers.   B.   Porpoises.
    C.   Nuisances.   D.   Self-propelled marine vehicles.

Mammals: Sea Creatures—Dolphins Answers

1. **B. Dorsal fin.** To someone who is not familiar with dolphins, its dorsal fin looks very much like a shark. People swimming at beaches have occasionally been frightened when a dolphin swam too close to shore.

2. **A. Keeps one eye open.** A dolphin is a mammal. This means that it needs to breathe air. If it would fall asleep in the middle of the ocean, one would think that it would sink and drown, but it doesn't. A dolphin's bone and body structure and its ability to hold a great deal of oxygen in its body make a dolphin very buoyant. In other words, it floats easily. So when it sleeps, it doesn't sink, but floats just below the surface of the water. It periodically pushes up to the surface so it can take a breath through its blowhole. In addition, it sleeps with one-half of its brain at a time and with one eye open. It does this because it has to surface so frequently for air. With its one open eye, it is able to keep track of the size of the waves. A dolphin is able to rest this way throughout the day as it switches the side of the brain it shuts down and rests.

3. **C. Play practical jokes.** Dolphins are playful creatures. All dolphins, young and old, have fun chasing and tossing seaweed to each other. They enjoy interacting with other dolphins, other creatures in the sea, and even humans. Sailors have observed dolphins sneak up behind a pelican, grab its tail feathers, and quickly swim away.

4. **A, B, C, D.** If you chose any answer, you are correct. Dolphins may have the best hearing in the entire animal kingdom, in spite of the fact that their ear holes are not much larger than a dot. In addition to hearing through their ears, dolphins receive sounds through their jawbones and heads and by the vibrations that pass into the tiny bones of their inner ears.

5. **A. Bats.** Both bats and dolphins use sound in order to find food and avoid predators. Water is sometimes not very clear, so dolphins make sounds that travel underwater, bounce off something, and then return to the dolphins. This process is called **echolocation**. In other words, they are able to use an **echo** to **locate** something.

6. **B. Pods**. A pod usually has a dozen or more dolphins.

7. **B. Larger.** While the brain of the bottlenose dolphin is larger than a human brain, the part concerned with intelligence is not.   .

8. **A. Give the baby a time out.** A mother dolphin will punish a baby by swimming over to it and holding it tightly for a few minutes.

9. **A. Is pink.** There are four or five species of small dolphins that live in the rivers of South America and Asia. River dolphins have a different appearance than the more common bottlenose dolphins. River dolphins have long beaks and rounded foreheads. River dolphins do not jump out of the water as do their marine cousins. They feed off of crustaceans and bottom-feeding fish. In order to navigate in the muddy waters, they use echolocation, since their eyes are small and not as keen as other species. The Amazon river dolphin's skin varies from dark gray to bright pink. While there are other dolphins that may have pink patches, some Amazon river dolphins are completely pink.

10. **D. Self-propelled marine vehicles.** For more than 25 years, about 100 Atlantic bottlenose dolphins have been in the navy. They are based at the Naval Command, Control, and Ocean Surveillance Center in San Diego, California. They are trained to find, mark, and recover objects in the ocean. Some have even seen war duty. In 1971, a team of dolphins was sent to Vietnam to guard the U.S. fleet. In 1987, six dolphins were sent to the Persian Gulf to protect the navy's floating command post.

Name: _____ Date: _____

Mammals: Other Sea Mammals

Directions: Circle the letter of the correct answer(s).

1. The world's smallest seal lives in:
   - A. Siberia.
   - B. The Sahara Desert.
   - C. The Red Sea.
   - D. Peoria, Illinois.

2. A warm winter in the Arctic may result in a harp seal pup:
   - A. Growing twice as fast.
   - B. Moving to land.
   - C. Turning black.
   - D. Drowning.

3. How many wives may male sea lions have?
   - A. 1
   - B. 20
   - C. 50
   - D. 100

4. Scientists are able to tell the age of some whales and some seals by looking at:
   - A. Their tails.
   - B. Their eyes.
   - C. Cross sections of their teeth.
   - D. The barnacles on their skin.

5. For what does a seal use its teeth?
   - A. To catch its prey
   - B. To cut its prey
   - C. To chew its prey
   - D. To grind its prey

6. A group of sea lions in the water is called a:
   - A. School.
   - B. Raft.
   - C. Pride.
   - D. Congery.

7. Seals and sea lions enjoy:
   - A. Surfing.
   - B. Showering.
   - C. Sunbathing.
   - D. Moonbathing.

8. In order to cool off, seals and sea lions:
   - A. Fan themselves.
   - B. Put ice under their flippers.
   - C. Eat snow cones.
   - D. Cover themselves with snow.

9. Scientists believe that seals share the same ancestors as:
   - A. Beavers.
   - B. Jackals.
   - C. Mackerels.
   - D. Sea snakes.

10. Seals and sea lions are very similar, so how do you tell them apart? A simple way is to look at their:
    - A. Blubber.
    - B. Ears.
    - C. Flippers.
    - D. Whiskers.

Name: _____ Date: _____

Mammals: Other Sea Mammals (cont.)

11. Which of the following is *not* a function of a sea lion's whiskers?
    A. To locate fish   B. To strain krill
    C. To balance objects on its nose   D. To aid in navigation

12. The U.S. Navy has trained sea lions to be:
    A. Lifeguards.   B. Sentries.
    C. Torpedoes.   D. Compasses.

13. The scientific name for a walrus is *Odobenus rosmarus*. It is taken from Latin and means:
    A. Large-toothed fish.   B. Mustache fish.
    C. Large seal.   D. Tooth-walking seahorse.

14. The polar bear is a predator of the walrus. Polar bears have been observed trying to catch a walrus by:
    A. Pretending to be a pile of snow. B. Throwing ice at it.
    C. Using a fish as bait.   D. Pretending to be hurt.

15. Legend has it that when sailors saw a manatee or dugong, they thought it was:
    A. A sea monster.   B. A mermaid.
    C. A sea spirit.   D. Neptune.

16. The manatee and the dugong are the only sea mammals that:
    A. Live in fresh water.   B. Are endangered.
    C. Are vegetarians.   D. Sleep on land.

17. Some people use manatees and dugongs as:
    A. Farmers.   B. Lawnmowers.
    C. Bulldozers.   D. Soldiers.

18. Manatees are mostly injured by:
    A. Killer whales.   B. Alligators.
    C. Boats.   D. Hunters.

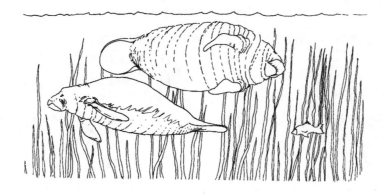

Mammals: Other Sea Mammals Answers

1. **A. Siberia.** The world's smallest seal lives in Lake Baikal, a large, freshwater lake in Siberia. Strangely enough, it is located about 1,000 miles from the sea. Why did seals decide to live in this remote location? Scientists have wondered about this for years. The most likely answer is that they originally lived in the Arctic Ocean during the Ice Age, and as the glaciers grew to the south, the seals went with them and found the lake. Eventually, the glaciers retreated, stranding the seals in the lake in which they live today. The lake freezes over in the winter, and the seals make holes in the ice in order to breathe. When it is time to give birth, the females climb out of these holes onto the ice and have their pups under the snow. The pups have long, white fur to keep them warm. They shed this coat in about eight weeks when they begin to swim.

2. **D. Drowning.** Females need to crawl out on the ice to give birth. If there is no ice, the pups drown.

3. **B. 20.** Male sea lions are called bulls and are much larger than the females, which are called cows. On the beach, where the sea lions go to breed, it is very crowded. Every adult bull tries to build a "harem" with as many cows as he can. He does this by barking and trying to scare off other males who might try to steal cows from his harem. If frightening them doesn't work, there will be a fight, and only the biggest and strongest will be able to build a large harem and mate. These sea lion harems are really family groups that include a bull and up to 20 cows and their young. The bull protects its harem. There is not just one harem on the beach, there are many. The area where the sea lions congregate to mate and give birth is called a **rookery,** and the harems are referred to as **colonies**.

4. **C. Cross sections of their teeth.** Just as a scientist is able to tell the age of a tree by counting the rings, so can he tell the age of some seals and some whales by the number of rings on their teeth. Of course, getting a tooth to count the number of its rings is the tricky part.

5. **A. To catch its prey.** A seal does not use its teeth to cut, grind, or chew its prey.

6. **B. Raft.**

7. **C. Sunbathing.** Seals enjoy lying in the sun in order to warm up.

8. **A. Fan themselves.** When seals lie out in the sun, they become overheated easily because of their excellent insulation. In order to cool off, they fan themselves with their front flippers. Sometimes they will bury their flippers in the cool wet sand. When elephant seals become too warm as they are basking in the sun, they toss cool sand on top of their backs.

9. **B. Jackals.** Scientists believe that seals evolved from a creature that looked like a dog and share the same ancestors as a jackal.

10. **B. Ears.** Both are marine mammals and part of a group of animals called **pinnipeds**, which means "wing foot" or "feather foot." Both have flippers, blubber, and whiskers. They both eat fish and spend each day in the ocean trying to find food. So how do they differ? One important difference is their ears. A seal has just tiny openings for its ears, while a sea lion has a small ear flap on each side of its head. There are other differences, of course. Sea lions can rotate their hind flippers forward, enabling them to scoot along the beach; seals are unable to do this. Once out of the water, seals have to wiggle, roll, or slide.

Mammals: Other Sea Mammals Answers (cont.)

11. **B. Strain krill.** The ocean can be a very dark place, making it difficult to find food and to get around. But sea lions have a tool that helps them with these two important tasks—their whiskers. Their whiskers are long and loosely attached to their upper lips. They contain nerve fibers, which make them sensitive and able to rotate around, "feeling" changes in the currents. They pick up vibrations in the water, helping them to detect the location of fish and aid in navigation. The whiskers of a sea lion are so effective in picking up vibrations of fish that a blind sea lion is still able to hunt fish. The whiskers are also important to the sea lions that perform in circuses and water shows. Without the whiskers, sea lions would be unable to balance balls on their noses. As the ball spins, the whiskers touch the ball, and if the ball begins to tip, the sea lion adjusts its position.

12. **B. Sentries.** The navy is concerned that terrorists may use divers to fasten explosives to the bottoms of ships. Sea lions have excellent underwater directional hearing and are able to see in near-darkness. This makes them invaluable in detecting terrorists who plan underwater attacks. The sea lions carry a clamp in their mouths, and if they see a diver approaching a ship, they sneak up behind him and put the clamp on the diver's leg. Then the sailors onboard haul the diver out of the water.

13. **D. Tooth-walking seahorse.**

14. **B. Throwing ice at it.** Russians have observed polar bears sneaking up on walruses and throwing chunks of ice at them. Another predator of the walrus is the killer whale. Killer whales will ram ice floes, trying to knock the walruses off and into the sea where they can be eaten. Killer whales will also work together by rounding up a group of walruses, much like cowboys round up cows, and then the killer whales will take turns swimming through the herd of walruses with their mouths open, catching whatever they can.

15. **B. A mermaid.** Manatees are usually brown or gray and have heavy, tapered bodies with a flat tail. They have flippers on the front of their bodies, but not in the back. Dugongs are similar to the American manatee but are found in Australia, Madagascar, Africa, in Asia, and in other parts of the world.

    A mermaid is a legendary marine creature with the head and upper body of a beautiful woman and the tail of a fish. It is hard to believe that anyone could mistake a manatee or a dugong for a beautiful woman, but if you were at a distance when one suddenly popped out of the surface of the ocean and you had been at sea for months, who knows?

16. **C. Are vegetarians.**

17. **B. Lawnmowers.** Since manatees and dugongs are vegetarians and eat tremendous amounts of vegetation each day, they have sometimes been used as underwater lawnmowers. In other words, they are kept in locations where it is necessary to keep vegetation at a minimum. Some of these locations would include waterways and dams where weeds and excessive plant life might lessen their effectiveness.

18. **C. Boats.** Manatees do not have any enemies in nature. In previous years, manatees were hunted for their delicious meat, oil, and hide. They were easy prey because they are gentle animals that move very slowly. As a result, the manatee population has decreased dramatically. There are now laws that protect this interesting creature. Manatees are often hurt by the propeller blades of boats. They inhabit the same waters as fishermen and sportsmen, and because they move so slowly, there are often collisions. Many manatees survive these collisions but have scars to remind them of their encounters.

Name: _____ Date: _____

Olympics in the Animal World

The Olympic Games had their origins in Greece over 3,500 years ago. At first it was just a single race. Over the years, more events such as longer races, wrestling, boxing, javelin throwing, discus throwing, the long jump, pentathlon, and others were added. The Olympics were discontinued by the Romans, but the modern games began again in 1896. These athletic games were designed to determine the strongest, fastest, and most skilled athletes in the whole world. But humans represent only a small percentage of all of the creatures on Earth. What if the Olympics truly represented the best athletes in the world? Who would be the best? All creatures are considered eligible for this contest, not just mammals.

Directions: Circle the letter of the animal that would have the best chance of winning each event.

1. **Sprinting** (short, fast races) were the first Olympic events. They still are among the most popular Olympic events.
   A. Racehorse   B. Cheetah
   C. Deer   D. Greyhound

2. **High jumping and broad jumping** would be interesting events because of the different sizes of the participants. Each participant's size would be taken into consideration. In other words, a bigger animal would be expected to jump higher and farther than a smaller animal.
   A. Grasshopper   B. Kangaroo
   C. Jumping spider   D. Flea

3. **Swimming.** Which animal would win speed-swimming?
   A. Sea turtles   B. Penguins
   C. Dolphins   D. Sailfish

4. **Diving.** While human divers are judged on the gymnastic flips and turns they make as they leave the board or platform and enter the water, animal athletes would be judged on how deep they dive and how long they stay under the water. It would not include those creatures that spend their entire lives at great depths. By and large, these animals do not dive. They stay at the bottom of the ocean. Instead, diving medals should be awarded to mammals who breathe air above the water and then dive deep into the ocean and stay under for a long time.
   A. Bottlenose dolphin   B. Seal
   C. Sperm whale   D. Penguin

5 **Sailing.** This would include only those creatures that use the wind to move them over the water.
   A. Portuguese man-of-war B. Flyingfish
   C. Stingray   D. Pond skater

103

Name: _____ Date: _____

Olympics in the Animal World (cont.)

6. **Rowing.**
   - A. Duck
   - B. Geese
   - C. Turtle
   - D. Backswimmer

7. **Gymnastics.** The word *gymnastics* is taken from a Greek word that means "to exercise naked." This may seem like a strange name, but in ancient Greece, male athletes exercised naked in a gymnasium. Some of these exercises became part of the Olympic Games, although some of the gymnastic events such as boxing, wrestling, and track and field later became separate events. Today's Olympic gymnastics include floor exercises, vaulting, pommel horse, rings, balance beam, horizontal bars, and the high bar.
   - A. Spider monkey
   - B. Baboon
   - C. Gorilla
   - D. Chimpanzee

8. **Weightlifting.**
   - A. Ant
   - B. Rhinoceros beetle
   - C. Gorilla
   - D. Elephant

9. **Marathon.** (long-distance race)
   - A. Sperm whales
   - B. Arctic terns
   - C. Eels
   - D. Monarch butterflies

10. Which animal would you think would win the decathlon? Explain your answer.

    _____

    _____

    _____

    _____

Olympics in the Animal World Answers

1. **B. Cheetah.** Deer can sprint between 35–40 miles per hour, depending on the species. The racehorse can reach speeds of slightly over 40 miles per hour. Greyhounds run about 39 miles per hour. Cheetahs can attain speeds of 60 miles per hour.

2. **D. Flea.** The kangaroo is the largest marsupial and can hop at 37 miles per hour. While it is not common, there are cases of frightened kangaroos jumping 10 feet. It is able to do this because of its strong legs and long, elastic Achilles tendons in its ankles. The jumping spider, which is less than 1/2 inch long, can jump 4 inches. What makes this feat even more incredible is that the spider does not have muscles. In order to jump, the jumping spider fills its bent legs with blood very rapidly. The legs straighten out, enabling the spider to leap and catch its prey. The grasshopper is able to jump 50 times the length of its body, which is incredible. However, the flea would be the champ. It can jump 130 times its height. That would be like a six-foot man jumping 780 feet. That would be high enough to jump over an office building. When the flea jumps, it is traveling at 20 times the speed of a rocket.

3. **D. Sailfish.** Sea turtles move very slowly when walking, but surprisingly fast when they swim. They can swim at about 21 miles per hour. While penguins are awkward on land, they are also fast and graceful once they get into the water. It is possible for penguins to swim at 24 miles per hour when they are near the surface. They swim and jump out of the water when they are moving at this tremendous speed. They use their wings as oars and their feet as rudders. But the gold medal goes to the sailfish, who is able to swim over 65 miles per hour. That is as fast as a person drives a car on the highway.

4. **C. Sperm whale.** First place goes to the sperm whale, which weighs 70 tons and is capable of diving 10,000 feet below the surface of the ocean and staying there for two hours before it comes up to breathe again. There are seals that are able to dive over 4,000 feet and stay under for an hour. This is the maximum. Many seals only dive to about 900 feet and stay under for only a few minutes. Bottlenose dolphins can dive to about 1,000 feet. The king penguin can dive 900 feet and can stay down for 20 minutes.

5. **A. Portuguese man-of-war**. Pond skaters are sometimes called water-striders. They are thin, dark insects with long legs. Their bodies and legs are covered in small hairs, which enable the pond skaters to walk on the surface of the water. While the wind sometimes moves them across the surface, they don't really sail because they are not really in the water; they are on top of it. The flyingfish does not really sail either. Although it can reach speeds of almost 40 miles per hour when it jumps out of the water, it doesn't sail. It swims very fast in the water and then jumps out and glides for about 1,000 yards before it descends into the water. The Portuguese man-of-war looks like a glob of blue jelly. In fact, many call it a jellyfish, but it isn't. Actually, a single Portuguese man-of-war is a colony of many animals that cling together. The man-of-war has a gas-filled bladder that sticks above the surface of the water and enables it to float. This bladder acts like a sail and pushes the animal along. It would win the gold medal.

6. **C. Turtle**. Ducks and geese are able to travel very quickly through the water using their webbed feet. However, they don't actually row; they paddle. They probably would do well in another event such as kayaking. The remaining possibilities—the insect called the backswimmer and the sea turtle would be eligible since they both row in order to travel. The backswimmer is a waterbug that was given the name *backswimmer* because it swims on its back near the surface of the water. It has long hind legs that are shaped like oars and are used to propel

Olympics in the Animal World Answers (cont.)

itself. First place for rowing would go to the marine (sea) turtle. A sea turtle's foot is a foot without toes; it is shaped like an oar. It is able to row over 21 miles per hour and has the strength to travel very long distances.

7. **A. Spider monkey.** The gorilla would certainly be strong enough, but not graceful enough to win a medal in this event. Baboons are also strong, but since they spend most of their time on the ground, they could not really hope to compete in this event with those that spend most of their time in trees. Chimpanzees are great gymnasts. They would excel in floor exercise, but like the baboon, could not compete with monkeys on any of the equipment such as the rings or bars. The winner would be the spider monkey. New World monkeys—those from South America—spend their time in the trees. Spider monkeys have a *prehensile* tail, and their feet are more like hands, so the monkey can perform all sorts of athletic stunts in the trees.

8. **B. Rhinoceros beetle.** Gorillas, orangutans, and even chimpanzees are very strong. But the elephant is even stronger. If the weight-lifting contest were for the animal that could lift the *largest number of pounds,* the elephant would surely win. However, most insects are very strong when their size is considered. One of the strongest animals is the ant, which can carry items that weigh 50 times heavier than its body weight. However, the rhinoceros beetle is able to lift 850 times its weight. This would be like a 200-pound man carrying 170,000 pounds.

9. **The winner of the marathon would depend on how it was judged.** Would the gold medal go to the creature that traveled the farthest or to the creature that traveled a great distance over a difficult course? If you think the creature that traveled the farthest should win, the Arctic tern, a bird, would be declared the winner. Terns breed in the Arctic and spend their winters in the Antarctic. This journey covers 21,750 miles each year. This bird spends about ten months of the year in the air.

    Probably the most difficult, extended journey would be that of the larvae of the eel. The Sargassso Sea is the spot to which eels from North America, Europe, and the Mediterranean go to mate, spawn, and then die. The Sargasso Sea is located in the central North Atlantic Ocean, between the West Indies and the Azores. The eel larvae will instinctively make the journey back to its respective country in America and Europe. That journey is up to 3,000 miles and can take three years. It does not feed as it travels. It lives on the store of fat in its body.

    There are other animals that travel great distances. The gray whale migrates along the Pacific Coast each year. It travels from the Arctic to Baja, California, and then back again. That is a distance of 5,000–6,000 miles one way. The North American monarch butterfly migrates 2,000 miles south in September in order to spend the winter in Mexico. In the spring, it returns. As it begins its northward trip each year, it stops from time to time to lay eggs and die. The hatching butterflies continue to travel to the north. In September, they repeat their migration to the south again.

10. **Answers will vary.** The decathlon is composed of ten events designed to see who is the overall best at running, jumping, and field events. Students should make a good argument for the animal they pick.

Name: _____   Date: _____

Logic Problem: Prairie Mammals

The Adams County Historical Society was given one hundred acres of woodlands about ten miles from the largest city in the county. They decided to create a zoo with animals that were native to the county before Europeans came. In order to save money, the Society asked community organizations to purchase mammals that will be included in the zoo and donate them to the Society. Three months later, six people, (Ms. Wu, Mr. Varner, Ms. Thompson, Ms. Alvarez, Mr. Harris, and Mr. Becks) each from a different organization (one is from the Garden Club), donated a different mammal, with no two having been donated on the same day.

Directions: Use the clues below and the grid on the next page to determine the day (Monday through Saturday) on which the donor from each organization made his or her donation. Also determine each donor's name, organization name, and the mammal that was donated. Write your final answers in the chart below.

Clues:

1. The man from Toastmasters (who didn't make his donation on Friday) made his donation three days after the man from the Genealogy Association.
2. No man made a donation immediately after another man.
3. The bison was donated the day after Ms. Alvarez's gift.
4. The coyote wasn't the first gift, but it was donated at some point before the black bear.
5. Ms. Thompson's donation did not come on Thursday, but immediately after Mr. Becks' donation, which was made at some point after the one from the Amateur Radio Club.
6. The bobcat arrived the day before the donation from the Ski Club, which was the day before the prairie dog arrived.
7. The river otter was a gift from the Community Theatre.
8. Mr. Varner made the first donation.
9. Ms. Wu is a representative of the Ski Club.
10. The river otter was the last gift donated.

Day	Donor's Name	Organization	Donation

107

Name: _____ Date: _____

Logical Problem: Prairie Mammals (cont.)

Directions: Use the grid below and the clues on the previous page to determine the day of donation, donor's name, name of organization, and mammal donated. Write your final answers in the chart on the previous page.

	Ms. Thompson	Ms. Alvarez	Mr. Harris	Ms. Wu	Mr. Varner	Mr. Becks	Prairie Dog	River Otter	Bison	Black Bear	Coyote	Bobcat	Garden Club	Toastmasters	Ski Club	Community Theatre	Genealogy Assn.	Radio Club
Monday																		
Tuesday																		
Wednesday																		
Thursday																		
Friday																		
Saturday																		
Garden Club																		
Toastmasters																		
Ski Club																		
Community Theatre																		
Genealogy Assn.																		
Radio Club																		

Name: _____ Date: _____

Logic Problem: Camel Races

In parts of the Middle East, camels are no longer being bred for their milk or meat or as beasts of burden. Instead, camels are being bred for their racing abilities. Camel racing in various mid-eastern countries is a traditional sport. Races were originally informal affairs held at weddings or special festivals. Today, however, there are special tracks for racing, specially bred camels, and formal races.

Directions: Alsarti Labib, Bistar Fadl, Safwan Jamal, Taleb Quasim, and Mousa Latif all owned camels that they entered and rode in a race. From the clues shown below, you are to figure out which rider rode which camel and the order in which they finished. Use the grid below to help organize the information. Place your final answers in the chart at the bottom of the page.

Clues:

1. The last camel to finish was Haji.
2. Jundi finished first.
3. Safwan Jamal rode Bash.
4. Taleb Quasim's camel finished fourth.
5. Bistar Fadl didn't finish second.
6. Alsarti Labib finished three places behind Barow.

	Gad	Barow	Jundi	Bash	Haji	1	2	3	4	5
Taleb Quasim										
Mousa Latif										
Bistar Fadl										
Safwan Jamal										
Alsarti Labib										
1					
2					
3					
4					
5					

Finish Order	Rider	Camel
1		
2		
3		
4		
5		

Name: _____ Date: _____

Logic Problem: Elephants

The zoo director and his assistant from the Springfield Zoo and the representatives from three other zoos waited patiently as the elephants they had just purchased were escorted off the plane from India. The new owners had all given the elephants new American first names, while keeping the original Indian names as their middle names. Of the four elephants, two are female who have been given the new names of Valerie and Savannah, and the other two are male and have been given the new names of Brendan and Christian. One elephant's Indian name was Manju.

Directions: Using the information above and the clues below, can you identify each elephant by its American name, Indian name, the zoo that purchased it, the director and assistant director of that zoo, and the order in which each came off the plane? Note: The directors are Don, Jim, Jeffery, and Adrian; and the assistant directors are Bonnie, Renée, Lisa, and Kelsey.

1. The Adamsville's female elephant wasn't the first elephant off the plane, nor was the male with the Indian name Chirag.
2. Adrian and his assistant and Bonnie and her director waited for their new males; the males did not exit one after the other.
3. The female with the Indian name Yamini exited the plane sometime before the New Madison's elephant and sometime after Christian.
4. Lisa's elephant, who isn't Savannah, came off just after Adrian's elephant.
5. Jim's female elephant got off sometime after Renée's female but sometime before the elephant male with the name Senajit.
6. The Jackson City's elephant exited sometime after Jeffery's.
7. Senajit was not the first male off of the plane.

Order	American	Indian	Zoo	Director	Asst. Director

Name: _____ Date: _____

Logic Problem: Primates

The order primates includes humans, apes, monkeys, and other creatures. Experts do not agree on how many primate species exist. The number depends on whether some closely related groups are considered primates or a different species. Some experts classify up to 350 species of primates, and others say there are only 190. Future DNA tests may give us more accurate numbers.

Directions: In the cages shown below are five different primates. Read the descriptions and clues of the primates and then write the primate's name in the box of the correct cage where that primate is placed.

Clues:

1. The primate, whose home is in Madagascar and is known for "stink fights," does not have a cage on its left as it looks out through the bars in front.
2. The largest and the rarest of the Asian apes is only next to an ape.
3. The largest ape is from Africa and so are the primates in the cages on either side of it.
4. The primates in cages 2 and 4 are not inhabitants of an island.
5. The primate that is the closest to humans genetically has a cage on either side of it.
6. One primate is found in the forests of Mexico, Central America, South America, Asia, Africa, Gibraltar, and even Spain. The various species of this primate may live in tropical forests, dry grasslands, and in mountains where there are heavy winter snows. These species have grasping hands, forward-facing eyes, highly developed brains, and most have tails.

Choose from the following primates: **Chimpanzee, Gorilla, Lemur, Monkey, Orangutan.**

Name: _____ Date: _____

Logic Problem: The African Water Hole

Water is just as important to animals as food. Many areas in Africa have watering holes, which the animals living in the surrounding area visit daily or by night. Impalas, warthogs, elephants, zebras, and wildebeests all visited a particular watering hole one night.

Directions: Use the following clues in order to discover the order in which the animals came to the watering hole.

1. The warthogs arrived before the wildebeests but behind the impalas.
2. The elephants arrived before the warthogs but behind the impalas.
3. The impalas did not arrive first.

1. _____   2. _____   3. _____

4. _____   5. _____

Logic Problem: Selling Zoo Mammals

The Middletown Zoo was having financial problems and had to sell several of its mammals to other zoos. The zoo decided to sell a hippopotamus, giraffe, and lemur. Each of the mammals was placed on a train to a different zoo.

Directions: Use the clues below to determine which mammal was sent to which zoo and the order in which the trains left the station.

Clues:

1. The hippopotamus didn't take the train to Quincy.
2. The giraffe didn't take the train to Pittsfield.
3. The lemur didn't take the Griggsville train.
4. The Quincy train left before the giraffe's train.
5. The Pittsfield train didn't leave first.

	Quincy	Pittsfield	Griggsville
Hippopotamus			
Giraffe			
Lemur			
Train left first			
Train left second			
Train left third			

Name: _____ Date: _____

Logic Problem: Lion Hunt

Over the period of several months, four lionesses named Ashaki, Deka, Eshe, and Meeka killed a number of animals so their prides could eat. Each lioness killed four different kinds of animals, and no type of animal was killed by more than two of the lionesses. The eight types of animals killed were antelope, gazelle, wildebeest, zebra, buffalo, hog, giraffe, and impala.

Directions: From the information above and the clues below, can you discover which four animals each lioness killed?

1. Ashaki killed a buffalo.
2. Deka killed an antelope, but not a hog.
3. Meeka killed an impala.
4. No lioness that killed a wildebeest also killed a gazelle.
5. Eshe was not one of the lionesses that killed a giraffe.
6. Only one of the lionesses that killed a wildebeest also killed a hog.
7. Ashaki did not kill a wildebeest or a hog.
8. Meeka and Eshe both killed a zebra.
9. No one killed both a giraffe and an impala.
10. Meeka did not kill a gazelle.

Lioness	Animal 1	Animal 2	Animal 3	Animal 4
Ashaki				
Deka				
Eshe				
Meeka				

Name: _____ Date: _____

Scientific Mysteries

Directions: Can you solve these mysteries? Spend some time researching the mysteries, and then write the answers on your own paper.

A Scientific Mystery: Pigs

In China many years ago, the people would shave pigs. Why?

A Scientific Mystery: Cows

Often when a calf is born, the farmer will make it swallow a magnet. Why?

A Scientific Mystery: Horses

If you have ever seen statues of soldiers sitting on a horse, you may have noticed that some statues have all four hooves of the horse on the ground, others have one hoof in the air, and others have two hooves in the air. Is there a significance to this, or does the sculptor just decide which looks best?

A Scientific Mystery: Automobiles

There is a part of a modern automobile that was originally designed for a horse and buggy. It was put on the buggy in order to keep the passengers from having mud splashed on them when the horses began running. The name that it was given then is still used today. What is it?

A Scientific Mystery: Bears

Bears are sometimes found on telephone poles. Why?

A Scientific Mystery: What Is The Animal?

What animal has a head like a giraffe, striped legs like a zebra, a body like an antelope, a tail like an ox, a neck like a horse, and a blue-black tongue two feet long?

A Scientific Mystery: What Do They Have in Common?

What do the following animals have in common: prairie dog, koala bear, flying fox, guinea pig, sea lion, and jackrabbit?

A Scientific Mystery: Giraffes

When most animals are born, the mother lies down so that the newborn comes into the world with little stress. This is not the case with giraffes. The mother giraffe stands, and the newborn falls six feet to the ground and lands on its head. Why doesn't a mother giraffe lie down while giving birth?

114

Answers to Activities

Mythbusters—Beavers (p. 9–10)

1. brown	2. pelt
3. mammals	4. eager beaver
5. lodge	6. Oregon
7. erosion	8. tail
9. water	10. teeth
11. New York	12. rodents
13. kit	14. webbed
15. fur	16. swimmers
17. colony	

Answer: BEAVERS ARE NOT BUSY.

Everyone has heard the phrase "Busy as a beaver." This old saying would lead one to believe that a beaver works very hard all the time. This isn't true. Beavers are very clever workers who are able to dam up streams in order to create a pond so that they can build their lodges. But busy all of the time? No. They spend more time playing rather than working. Al Milotte, who made a film about beavers for Disney, had trouble filming a beaver actually working. He had to watch them playing for several weeks before he saw them cut down a tree.

Collective Nouns for Mammals (p. 13)

1. Apes, Shrewdness	2. Baboons, Flange
3. Bears, Sleuth	4. Buffalo, Herd
5. Camels, Flock	6. Cats, Clutter
7. Cheetahs, Coalition	8. Chicks, Brood
9. Colts, Rag	10. Dolphins, Pod
11. Elk, Gang	12. Ferrets, Business
13. Foxes, Skulk	14. Giraffes, Tower
15. Greyhounds, Leash	16. Goats, Tribe
17. Gorillas, Band	18. Hamsters, Horde
19. Hippopotami, Bloat	20. Hogs, Drift
21. Jackrabbits, Husk	22. Kangaroos, Mob
23. Leopards, Leap	24. Lions, Pride
25. Monkeys, Troop	26. Ponies, String
27. Porpoises, School	28. Puppies, Litter
29. Rats, Colony	30. Rhinoceroses, Crash
31. Seals, Harem	32. Squirrels, Drey
33. Swine, Sounder	34. Tigers, Ambush
35. Wolves, Pack	36. Zebra, Zeal

Australian Coat of Arms Puzzle (p. 17)

Answer: NEITHER HAS THE CAPABILITY OF WALKING BACKWARDS

It is a commonly held belief that the kangaroo and the emu were selected for depiction on the Australian Coat of Arms because they, like the nation that was being forged, could only move forward.

A Fascinating Fact About a Mammal (p. 18)

1. blue whale	2. giraffe
3. fleece	4. kitten
5. elephant, walrus, boar	6. fox
7. Cayman, Fiji, Cook	8. Antarctica
9. tortoise	10. coyote
11. jaguar	12. armadillo
13. monkey, chimpanzee, gorilla	
14. ox, camel	15. herd
16. bat	
17. duck, goose, chicken, pig, sheep, cow	
18. seal	19. bamboo
20. opossum	21. pouch
22. Amazon, Nile, Mississippi	

Answer: A female kangaroo can produce two different kinds of milk at the same time when she is nursing youngsters of different ages.

Camel Puzzle (p. 21)

Answer: CAMELS WERE ONCE USED BY THE U.S. ARMY AS PACK ANIMALS.

There was once even a camel corps in the United States Army. Camels first came to this country in 1855 when Congress spent $30,000 to buy 33 camels to be used to explore the southwest. The army even hired Arabs to take care of the camels. Since the southwest is a dry, hot area, similar to the camels' natural home in the Middle East, it was thought that they would do well in the United States. They did perform well, even though they didn't like the rocky soil. However, the men in the army hated the camels so much because of their behavior that the camel corps was disbanded. Some of the camels were sold, and the others were set free in the Arizona territory. Most of the wild camels were killed by sportsmen.

Amazing Mammals Fact Puzzle (p. 26–27)
Answer: ELEPHANTS SOMETIMES GO SNOR-KELING.

While it does not seem possible, when an elephant wants to wade across high water that is above its head, it is able to raise its trunk and use it as a snorkel.

Odd Mammal Fact From History (p. 36–37)

1. antelope
2. squirrel
3. tiger
4. baboon
5. kangaroo
6. otter
7. zebra
8. lion
9. giraffe
10. gazelle
11. panda
12. monkey
13. aardvark
14. elephant
15. rabbit
16. manatees
17. dingo
18. camel
19. armadillo

Answer: PUT ON TRIAL AND HANGED

It may be hard for us to believe, but from the later Middle Ages until the eighteenth century, some people in Europe felt that animals could commit crimes. When an animal or animals were accused of a crime, they were put on trial, and if convicted, they were punished and sometimes executed. The animals that were executed most often were pigs. One well-known case occurred in 1266 in France and involved a pig who was convicted of killing a child. The pig was burned to death. Another pig that was found guilty was dressed in men's clothes and publicly executed.

While pigs were the animals most commonly tried in court, they were not the only ones. Dogs, cats, wolves, and other animals who were accused of crimes found themselves in jail with humans as they waited for their trials to begin.

Creatures that destroyed crops or property or that ate grain were also subject to criminal prosecution. Locusts, grasshoppers, caterpillars, beetles, snakes, birds, mice, rats, and termites were prosecuted during the Middle Ages and later. Often these natural pests were not tried in a regular court but were tried by the Church. Here is an example of how it worked for a group of moles in 1519 in Italy who were accused of damaging crops. The charges were first read in the fields to the moles. They were commanded to show up for a trial at a certain date. A lawyer was appointed to represent them. The day of the trial, the defendants did not show up. This was common. Wild creatures seldom came to their trials

on their own. Often when the accused animal did not show up for its trial, it was automatically found guilty and punished. But if the animals had a good lawyer, they still could have a trial. As the trial for the moles progressed, there were witnesses who testified to how much damage was caused by the moles. The moles were found guilty of damaging the crops and were ordered to leave the fields at once. The moles' lawyer asked the moles be given protection from cats, dogs, and other enemies as they left. The judge granted them that. Then the lawyer asked that the very young moles be given an extra fourteen days to leave. The judge also granted this request. Then he said that after the additional time, all moles had to leave or would be killed. Guess what? The moles refused to leave as they were commanded, and the sentence was carried out. Before they were killed, however, the church performed a ritual that was similar to an excommunication.

The last known case of an animal being tried for a crime happened in Switzerland, in 1906.

The question many ask today is, "Why?" Probably part of the reason was just revenge and the belief that people thought Satan was acting through animals when they killed or hurt someone. For this reason, guilty animals were even excommunicated by the Catholic Church. Another reason to punish animals came from the Bible. In medieval times, people took literally the passage in *Exodus* that says, "If an ox gore a man or a woman that they die, then the ox shall be surely stoned, and his flesh shall not be eaten; but the owner of the ox shall be quit." Exodus, xxi: 28.

Because of this Bible passage, the flesh of an executed animal was not eaten. Their bodies were usually buried, often under the gallows or in the same spot that human criminals were buried.

What's the Difference? (p. 40)

1. RABBIT—HARE: Hares are larger than rabbits and have longer back legs and longer ears. Hares are born with a full coat of fur and with their eyes open. A hare's mother just drops the newborn on the bare ground. A young hare is called a leveret. Hares prefer to live alone and hide among plants.

Rabbits are smaller than hares, and when they are born, they have no fur and are blind. The mother rabbit makes a nest with grass and materials and puts a layer of her own hair over the nest. The young are called bunnies. Rabbits live in groups and live in burrows underground.

2. BACTRIAN—DROMEDARY: Asian camels come from the deserts of China and Mongolia. They are called Bactrian camels. They have heavy, shaggy coats in the winter and are able to withstand both cold and hot temperatures. They have two humps on their backs. The dromedary, on the other hand, comes from East and North Africa and has a coat that is not as heavy, so they cannot withstand the cold as well as the Bactrian camel. A dromedary has one hump.

3 MOOSE—ELK: Moose are the largest animals in the Deer family. They are over six feet tall and weigh over 1,000 pounds. They live in the northern United States and in Canada. In Europe and Asia, moose are called elk. In North America, there is another kind of deer known as the North American elk. It is also called a wapiti. The wapiti, or North American elk, is a bit smaller than a moose, and its antlers look like tree branches.

4. CARIBOU—REINDEER: Reindeer and caribou are different names for the same species. They are a large, antlered animal related to deer and elk. Caribou live in Alaska, Canada, Scandinavia, and Russia. In Europe, they are usually called reindeer, while they are called caribou in North America.

5. BAT—BIRD: Bats are mammals. Birds aren't. All birds have feathers. Bird wings are composed of feathers. Bats' wings have hands and arms with skin membranes that serve as wings.

6. PORPOISE—DOLPHIN: Even though dolphins and porpoises live in the ocean, both are mammals. They are not fish. They have lungs and breathe air. They don't have gills. While they are similar in appearance, there are obvious differences that even a person who is not a scientist can see. Porpoises are smaller than dolphins. They are about seven feet long, while dolphins are often ten feet long. Porpoises are plump, while dolphins are thin. The dorsal fin, which is the fin on the back, on a porpoise is shaped like a triangle. On the dolphin, it is shaped like a wave. The teeth of the porpoise are shaped like a spade. A dolphin's teeth are shaped like a cone. A dolphin has a beak, or an area by the mouth, called a rostrum. A porpoise lacks a rostrum or a beak.

7. RAT—MOUSE: Rats and mice are closely related, but a mouse is not just a baby rat. A rat is a medium-sized rodent with a long, thin tail. Rats have coarse, dull-colored fur. They have pointed snouts, long tails, and large ears. A mouse is a small rodent that belongs to the same family as the rat.

8. BUFFALO—BISON: When Europeans came to North America and saw the large herds of a large, shaggy, brown animal, they called them buffalo. This name became popular, and it is the one we still use today. But it is not accurate. The animal we call a buffalo in the United States is not really a buffalo. It is more closely related to the European bison and the Canadian woods bison. Buffalos live in Asia or Africa. They are large, dark brown or black hoofed animals, with fringed ears that droop and with large curved horns. The water buffalo is an example.

9. WEASEL—ERMINE: The weasel and the ermine are the same animal. In winter, its coat is white, and it is known as an ermine. When the weather is warm, its coat is brown, and it is called a weasel.

10. MANATEE—DUGONG: The main difference between manatees and dugongs is the shapes of their tails. The manatee's tail is paddle-shaped and rounded like a spoon. The dugong's tail is shaped like a fluke, similar to that of a whale. Manatees live in rivers and coastal waters. Their mouths are designed to allow them to eat a wide variety of vegetation. Dugongs live in coastal waters, and their mouths are designed to feed mainly on sea grass and other water plants.

11. SEAL—SEA LION: Seals and sea lions look very much alike, but sea lions have ear flaps, while seals have only openings for their ears. Sea lions are able to move their back flippers underneath their bodies in order to help them move on land. Seals can't.

Animals' Homes Answers (p. 47)
1. A beaver lives in a lodge.
2. A baby kangaroo lives in a pouch.
3. An otter lives in a holt.
4. A bat lives in a roost.
5. A rabbit lives in a warren.
6. An ant lives in an ant hill.
7. A squirrel lives in a drey.
8. A fox lives in a den.
9. A termite lives in a termite mound.
10. A spider lives in a web.
11. A bee lives in a hive.
12. A mole lives in a hole.

13. A hare lives in a form.
14. A badger lives in a sett.
15. A crocodile lives in a nest.
16. A hermit crab lives in a snail shell.

Find The Mammals (p. 48)

1. Such are the facts of the case.
2. Supersize brakes stop big trucks.
3. Susan is such a chatterbox.
4. "You should tap irregular pickets," the boss explained.
5. There are approximately ten million bad germs in every sneeze.
6. He cannot be arrested in the chapel.
7. She visited the pyramids, which are enormous edifices.
8. The school decided to establish rewards for good attendance.
9. Wake up and attack the day.
10. A person should be happy in one's lot in life.
11. To be a rich man and have millions is a fantasy for many.
12. Jeb is on the job at 8:00 every day.
13. The park ranger would release a little chipmunk each day.
14. Cory X. Welk, from nearby Akron, was perfect.
15. James Stiger made an enormous effort to win.
16. People who win the lottery tend to brag.
17. Tom would always lose all patience.
18. No one wants to be average.
19. He was not terribly impressed with the cheap eraser.
20. Heraklion is the capital of the island and the largest city on Crete.
21. The newspaper reporter made errors in his story.
22. The acrobat stopped, tottered, and then fell.
23. Cliff Oxman wore a beard.
24. "He is such a cruel kid," the teacher said.
25. Missing his favorite dessert was a harsh reward for bad behavior.
26. Whenever possible, he would grab bits of chocolate.
27. Don't debate each other.
28. "Both are graduates from separate colleges," the proud mother said.
29. He sheepishly asked for a vacation.
30. He was not terribly impressed with the game.
31. He was pleased with the girl who greeted him warmly.
32. You could tell he was obnoxious by the way he filled out the application.
33. The coward became rattled when he ate horseradish.
34. Only evil people murder others.
35. Nice people do good.

Baby Mammals (p. 51)

1. A baby cow is called a calf.
2. A baby bear is called a cub.
3. A baby deer is called a fawn.
4. A baby beaver is called a kit.
5. A baby cat is called a kitten.
6. A baby elephant seal is called a weaner.
7. A baby goat is called a kid.
8. A baby seal is called a pup.
9. A baby rabbit is called a bunny or kit.
10. A baby sheep is called a lamb.
11. A baby kangaroo is called a joey.
12. A baby pig is called a piglet.
13. A baby rat is called a pup.
14. A baby whale is called a calf.
15. A baby horse is called a foal.
16. A baby elephant is called a calf.
17. A baby fox is called a cub, pup, or kit.
18. A baby zebra is called a foal.
19. A baby hare is called a leveret.
20. A baby hedgehog is called a piglet or pup.
21. A baby monkey is called an infant.
22. A baby mouse is called a pinkie.
23. A baby echidna is called a puggle.

Mythbuster: Rodents (p. 60–62)

1. woodchuck	2. beaver
3. rodents	4. muskrat
5. pinky	6. rabbit
7. mouse	8. bat
9. groundhog	10. nuts
11. guinea pig	12. colony
13. porcupine	14. squirrels
15. mammals	16. gerbils
17. chipmunk	18. mole

Answer: CARRY BUBONIC PLAGUE.

The bubonic plague, also called the black death, killed 25 million people over a period of 300 years in Europe. The death rate was 90 percent for those who were infected. At that time, people thought, and some still do, that the disease was caused by Old English black rats. But it was not rats that carried the disease. It was transmitted by fleas, which carried the bacteria that caused the plague. The rats carried the fleas.

Dog Idioms (p. 67)

1. Put on the dog—To show off
2. A barking dog never bites— A person who talks a lot or makes a lot of noise about something won't actually do anything about it.
3. You can't teach an old dog new tricks—It is difficult for an older person to learn new skills.
4. Every dog has its day—Everyone, even unsuccessful people, has success at least once in his or her life.
5. Gone to the dogs—Something has gone very wrong and has lost all of its value.
6. Sick as a dog—Very sick
7. Underdog—Not the favorite to win
8. The tail wagging the dog—The follower is doing the leading, or the small part is controlling the whole thing.
9. In the doghouse—Facing punishment for doing something wrong
10. If you lie down with dogs, you will get up with fleas—If you associate with bad people, you will pick up their bad habits.
11. His bark is worse than his bite—Someone who talks or threatens won't actually do anything about it.
12. A dog and pony show—A planned show that is done in order to persuade or influence
13. Let sleeping dogs lie—Do not disturb someone or something that is not causing a problem.
14. Treat somebody like a dog—Treat them badly.

Cat Idioms (p. 70)

1. Looked like the cat that ate the canary—Smug; pleased with oneself
2. The cat's pajamas—Something that is very good; the best
3. Looks like something the cat dragged in—Someone who is untidy or dirty
4. Raining cats and dogs—A heavy downpour
5. More than one way to skin a cat—There are many different ways of doing the same thing.
6. When the cat's away, the mice will play—When no one of authority is around, people will misbehave.
7. Playing cat and mouse—Teasing or fooling someone
8. Has the cat got your tongue—Unable to speak
9. Fight like cats and dogs—Fighting often or with great intensity
10. Let the cat out of the bag—To reveal a secret
11. Grin like a Cheshire cat—To smile so widely as to show all one's teeth
12. Not enough room to swing a cat—A small space
13. A catnap—A short nap
14. Curiosity killed the cat—Sometimes being too curious is not a good thing.

Horse Idioms (p. 75)

1. Lock the barn door after the horse has gone—To take action too late
2. Get on one's high horse—To become offended or angry in a superior way
3. Change horses in midstream—Change an opinion in the middle of something
4. Put the cart before the horse—To do things in the wrong order
5. Don't look a gift horse in the mouth—Don't question the value of a gift.
6. You can lead a horse to the water, but you can't make it drink—You can make it easy for a person to do something, but you cannot force them to do it.
7. Beating a dead horse—To keep trying to get satisfaction from something that cannot give it.
8. Horse of a different color—A different matter
9. Hold your horses—Wait
10. Straight from the horse's mouth—Information from a person closely concerned with the subject.
11. Eat like a horse—To eat a lot.
12. Horse sense—Common sense
13. Horseplay—To fool around

14. A dark horse—Unknown quantity, or somebody about whom very little is known, or someone who unexpectedly succeeds

Farm Animal Idioms (p. 80–81)

1. Take the bull by the horns—Confront a problem without hesitation
2. A sacred cow—Something that should not be criticized or discussed
3. Like a bull in a china shop—A clumsy person
4. Like a red cape to a bull—Infuriating
5. Hit the bull's-eye—A perfect shot
6. Bullheaded—Stubborn
7. Till the cows come home—A long time
8. A cash cow—A business, activity, or product that makes a lot of money
9. Kill the goose that lays the golden egg—To destroy, often by greed, a person's source of profit
10. A scapegoat—Someone who is blamed for a mistake or crime for which someone else is responsible
11. Get your goat—To irritate someone
12. In two shakes of a lamb's tail—A very short time
13. Separate the sheep from the goats—Separate the good from the bad
14. Chicken feed—A small amount of money
15. A chicken with its head cut off—To energetically move around doing things with no organization
16. Chickens come home to roost—The bad thing that someone did is resulting in bad things happening to him/her now.
17. Don't count your chickens before they are hatched—Do not expect good results from something until it actually happens.
18. Go to bed with the chickens—Go to bed early
19. To chicken out—To lose courage
20. A sitting duck—Defenseless
21. Get one's ducks in a row—Becoming prepared or organized
22. Like water off a duck's back—Has no effect
23. Take to it like a duck to water—To do something naturally and without difficulty
24. A cock-and-bull story—An unbelievable story
25. A wild goose chase—A chase after something or someone with no chance of success

Cow Puzzle (p. 82)

Answer: A PERSON CAN LEAD A COW UPSTAIRS BUT NOT DOWNSTAIRS

Mythbuster: Bats (p. 87–88)

1. bumble bee
2. mammals
3. echolocation
4. claws
5. feathers
6. rabies
7. bees
8. insects
9. roost
10. Antarctica
11. hibernate
12. cattle
13. flying
14. night
15. blood

Answer: BATS ARE NOT BLIND.

Many have good eyesight but use sound (echolocation) to fly in the dark. They are able to find very small insects in the dark. Other myths about bats are they get tangled in a person's hair. Not true. They avoid people. Another myth is they are related to mice, because they look like a mouse. But they are not rodents. Still another myth is that bats spread rabies. Like all mammals, they can contract rabies, but they do not get the disease any more often than other animals. Fewer people die from rabies transmitted by bats than die from dog bites or bee stings.

Logic Problem: Prairie Mammals (p. 107–108)

Mr. Varner made the first donation. Mr. Varner (a man) did not donate the bison (clue 3), coyote, black bear (clue 4), prairie dog (clue 6), or river otter (clue 10); he gave the bobcat. Since no man made a donation immediately after another man (clue 2), Mr. Becks and Mr. Harris must have made their donations on Thursday and Saturday. Mr. Becks must have made his donation on Thursday, since his donation immediately preceeded Ms. Thompson's donation, which wasn't made on Thursday (Clue 5). Ms. Thompson's donation couldn't have been made on Tuesday because it immediately followed Becks, not Varner (clue 5). By elimination, Ms. Thompson made her donation on Friday, and Mr. Harris, a representative of the Community Theatre, must have made his donation of the river otter (clues 7 and 10) on Saturday. The Ski Club made their donation on Tuesday (clue 6) by Ms. Wu (clue 9). The prairie dog arrived on Wednesday (clue 6). Since the bobcat was donated on Monday, the prairie dog on Wednesday, and the river otter on Saturday, the bison must have been donated on Thursday because it had to come after Ms. Alvarez's donation (clue 3). This means that the coyote arrived on Tuesday and the black bear on Friday (clue 4). Ms. Alvarez's gift was made on Wednesday (clue 3). Since Mr. Becks' donation was made at some point after the one from the Amateur Radio Club (clue 5), he must represent Toastmasters (clue 1), and Ms. Alvarez, who made her donation on Wednesday, must represent the Amateur Radio Club.

Answer:

Monday, Mr. Varner, Genealogy Association, bobcat

Tuesday, Ms. Wu, Ski Club, coyote

Wednesday, Ms. Alvarez, Amateur Radio Club, Prairie Dog

Thursday, Mr. Becks, Toastmasters, bison

Friday, Ms. Thompson, Garden Club, black bear

Saturday, Mr. Harris, Community Theatre, river otter

Logic Problem: Camel Races (p. 109)

Alsarti Labib finished three places behind Barow (clue 6), so he must have finished either fourth or fifth. But he couldn't have finished fourth, because Taleb Quasim's camel finished fourth. So Alsarti Labib must have finished last riding Haji (clue 1). Barow finished second since he finished three places before Haji (clue 6). Since Bistar Fadl didn't finish second (clue 5), and Safwan Jamal didn't ride Barow (clue 3), and Taleb Quasim's camel finished fourth (clue 4), then Mousa Latif must have ridden Barow and come in second. By elimination, this leaves Bistar Fadl riding Jundi for a first place finish. Since Safwan Jamal rode Bash (clue 3), and Taleb Quasim's camel finished fourth (clue 4), then Taleb must have ridden Gad and came in fourth place and Safwan Jamal rode Bash to a third-place finish.

Answer:

Bistar Fadl rode Jundi in first place.

Mousa Latif rode Barow in second place.

Safwan Jamal rode Bash in third place.

Taleb Quasim rode Gad in fourth place.

Alsarti Labib rode Haji in last place.

Logic Problem: Elephants (p. 110)

The males didn't exit consecutively (clue 2). Neither of the males—Chirag (clue 1) nor Senajit (clue 5)—got off first, so they must have exited in the following order: female, male, female, male. The female Yamini also wasn't first (clue 3), so Manju was, and Yamini was third. Senajit was not the first male off of the plane (clue 7), so Chirag must have exited second and Senajit last. The New Madison's elephant got off last, and Christian got off second (clue 3). Jim's female is Yamini (clue 5). This makes Renée's female Manju, and since Senajit is the last male, its American name must be Brendan, who was fourth off the plane. Chirag, then, is the second male, Christian. The Adamsville's female wasn't first (clue 1), so they must have purchased Yamini. The Jackson City elephant isn't first either (clue 6); neither is the New Madison elephant (clue 3). So, Springfield, by elimination, must have purchased the first elephant off the plane. Jeffery is the director of the Springfield Zoo (clue 6). Then, Lisa's elephant, who isn't Savannah, followed Adrian's (clue 4), who's a male (clue 2). Lisa's elephant, then, must be Valerie who was purchased by the Adamsville Zoo. Savannah, then, is the first elephant. Also by clue 4, Adrian's elephant is the second elephant, Christian. Bonnie has one of the new males but isn't assistant to Adrian (clue 2,); she's assistant to Don, and they have the fourth elephant. Kelsey, by elimination, is Jackson City's assistant director.

Answer:

First: Savannah, Manju, Springfield, Jeffery, and Renée

Second: Christian, Chirag, Jackson City, Adrian, and Kelsey

Third: Valerie, Yamini, Adamsville, Jim, and Lisa

Fourth: Brendan, Senajit, New Madison, Don, and Bonnie

Logic Problem: Primates (p. 111)

The lemur, from Madagascar, is in cage 5 (clue 1). The gorilla, the largest ape, must be in cage two or three since there are primates from Africa on either side of it (clue 3). But since the orangutan has only one cage next to it, which has an ape (clue 2), then the gorilla must be in the middle cage with the monkey on one side and the chimpanzee on the other. The chimpanzee, the primate that is the closest to humans genetically, must be in cage 2 because it is next to the gorilla in the center (clue 5), and the orangutan who is next to an ape (clue 2). This means that the orangutan must be in cage 1, and by elimination, this leaves cage four for the monkey, since it is from Africa (clue 3) and is next to the gorilla.

Answer:

1. Orangutan   2. Chimpanzee   3. Gorilla
4. Monkey   5. Lemur

Logic Problem: The African Watering Hole (p. 112)

Answer:

1. zebras   2. impalas
3. elephants   4. warthogs
5. wildebeests

Logic Problem: Selling Zoo Mammals (p. 112)

The giraffe did not go to Quincy (clue 4). It also did not go to Pittsfield (clue 2). So it must have gone to Griggsville. The hippopotamus did not go to Quincy (clue 1). So it must have gone to Pittsfield. This leaves the lemur that went to Quincy. The Pittsfield train wasn't first (Clue 5), and since the Quincy train left before the giraffe's train (clue 4), then the Quincy train must have left first.

Answer:

The lemur's train left first and was traveling to Quincy, then the giraffe's train left for Griggsville, so the hippopotamus's train left last and was traveling to Pittsfield.

Logic Problem: Lion Hunt (p. 113)

Since each lioness killed four different animals and no animal was killed by more than two of the lionesses (introduction), the only possibility is that each of the eight animals was killed by exactly two lionesses. Ashaki killed a buffalo (clue 1), Deka killed an antelope (clue 2), and Meeka killed an impala (clue 3). Meeka also killed a zebra, and so did Eshe (clue 8). Eshe did not kill a giraffe (clue 5); neither did Meeka (clue 9), so both Ashaki and Deka did. Also by clue 9, then, neither Ashaki nor Deka killed an impala, so the second one who did was Eshe. Neither Deka (clue 2) nor Ashaki (clue 7) killed a hog, so Meeka and Eshe both did. Again by clue 6, then, the two who killed a wildebeest were either Meeka or Eshe—but not both—and Deka. By clue 4, Deka did not kill a gazelle, and the two who did must have been Ashaki and either Meeka or Eshe; Meeka didn't (clue 10), so Eshe did, and Meeka killed a wildebeest. By elimination, Ashaki's fourth animal was an antelope, and Deka's was a buffalo.

Answer: (Animals can be in any order.)

Ashaki: Antelope, Gazelle, Buffalo, Giraffe
Deka: Antelope, Wildebeest, Buffalo, Giraffe
Eshe: Gazelle, Zebra, Hog, Impala
Meeka: Wildebeest, Zebra, Hog, Impala

A Scientific Mystery: Pigs (p. 114)

In China, live pigs were used like hot-water bottles to keep people warm in bed on cold nights. In order to keep the pig smooth and more comfortable for the person sleeping, the pigs were shaved first.

A Scientific Mystery: Cows (p. 114)

The purpose of the magnet is to attract the various kinds of metals such as nails, staples, tacks, and wire that the cow may ingest while grazing. Farmers call the practice of eating metal, hardware *disease*. When the animal is slaughtered, the butcher will remove the magnet as well as all the pieces of metal. The metal may be sold for scrap.

A Scientific Mystery: Horses (p. 114)

When all four of the horse's hooves are on the ground, it means that the rider died a natural death. One hoof in the air means that he died from wounds he received in action. If two hooves are raised, it means that the rider was killed while fighting a battle.

A Scientific Mystery: Automobiles (p. 114)

The area where the car's instrument panel is located is called a *dashboard*. When people rode in buggies, they were often splattered with mud that came from the horse's hooves when they began to go faster. So manufacturers of buggies began placing a *board* that stopped the mud from being splashed on the passengers when the horse began to *dash*.

A Scientific Mystery: Bears (p. 114)

When a bear hears the wires humming, he thinks it is the humming of bees. So he climbs the telegraph pole in hopes of finding the beehive and honey.

A Scientific Mystery: What Is The Animal? (p. 114)

The okapi. Okapis, which are relatives of the giraffe, live in Africa.

A Scientific Mystery: What Do They Have in Common? (p. 114)

They are not what their names imply.
The prairie dog is not a dog. It is a rodent.
The koala bear is not a bear. It is a marsupial.
The flying fox is not a fox. It is a bat.
The guinea pig is not a pig. It is a rodent.
The sea lion is not a lion. It is a marine mammal.
The jackrabbit is not a rabbit. It is a hare.

A Scientific Mystery: Giraffes (p. 114)

It takes so long for a mother giraffe to stand that if she would lie down to give birth, she would be exposed to predators.

Amazing Mammals Fact Sheet

Using science books, reference books, the Internet, or other reference sources, find some interesting facts about four mammals and write them here; include some pictures of the mammals. Perhaps your teacher can combine all of the class's pages into an "Interesting Mammals" book.

1. _____
   _____
   _____
   _____
   _____
   _____

2. _____
   _____
   _____
   _____
   _____
   _____

3. _____
   _____
   _____
   _____
   _____
   _____

4. _____
   _____
   _____
   _____
   _____
   _____

Bibliography

Amazing Animal Facts—by Jacqui Bailey, et al

Amazing Animals—by Gerald Legg

Amazing Animal Senses—by Atie Van Der Meer, Ron Van Der Meer

Amazing Animals Question & Answer Book—by Judy Braus, Jody Marshall, Joyce Altman, and Nancy Hitchner

Animal Fact/Animal Fable—by Seymour Simon

Animal Fact File—by Dr. Tony Hare

The Answer Book—by Mary Elting

The Beano Book of Amazing Facts—London: Kingfisher Books

The Big Book of Knowledge—A Paragon Publishing book

The Big Book of Questions and Answers—by Jane Parker Resnick, Rebecca L. Brambo, Tony Tallarico

The Book of Tell Me Why—by Arkady Leokum

Boyd's Book of Odd Facts—by L.M. Boyd

Did Mohawks Wear Mohawks—by Bruce Tindall and Mark Watson

Do Penguins Have Knees?—by David Feldman

Facts and Fallacies by Reader's Digest—A Dorling Kindersley Book

Fantastic Book of Comparisons—by Russell Ash

5087 Trivia Questions & Answers—by Marsha Kranes

Foul Facts of Our World: The Awful Truth—by Amber Grayson, Jamie Stokes, and Friend

Freaky Facts—Sterling Publishing Company

Fun Facts About Cats—Written and Illustrated by Richard Torregrossa

Isaac Asimov's Book of Facts—by Isaac Asimov

I Wonder Why Fish Don't Drown and Other Neat Facts about Underwater Animals—by Annabelle Donan

I Wonder Why Skunks Are So Smelly and Other Neat Facts about Mammals—by Deborah De Ford

The Little Giant Book of Animal Facts—by Glen Vecchione, et al

Not Many People Know That!—by Michael Caine

Odd Facts—by Will Eisner. Tempo/Grosset & Dunlap

1000 Facts on Animals: Mammals, Birds, Reptiles and Amphibians, Sea Creatures, Insects and Spiders—by John Farndon

The Original Trivia Treasury: 1,001 Questions for Competitive Play—by R. Wayne Schmittberger

Our Amazing World of Nature: Its Marvels and Mysteries—Reader's Digest

Quizzing: Everything You Always Wanted to Know but Didn't Know Where to Look (The Ultimate Trivia Book)—by Ranjit Thomas

Strange But True Facts—by Clifford Sawhney

Super Facts—by the Adelmans

10,000 Answers: The Ultimate Trivia Encyclopedia—by Stanley Newman, Hal Fittipaldi

Things You Know That Are Not So—by David Moshinsky

2201 Fascinating Facts—by David Louis

What Are Hyenas Laughing At, Anyway?—David Feldman

When Do Fish Sleep?—by David Feldman

Why Do Clocks Run Clockwise?—David Feldman